# UNDERSTANDING DRUGS

## Antidepressants and Antianxiety Drugs

# TITLES IN THE *UNDERSTANDING DRUGS* SERIES

Alcohol

Antidepressants and Antianxiety Drugs

Cancer Treatment Drugs

Cocaine and Crack

Ecstasy

Prescription Pain Relievers

Ritalin and Related Drugs

# UNDERSTANDING DRUGS

# Antidepressants and Antianxiety Drugs

Alan Hecht, D.C.

CONSULTING EDITOR
DAVID J. TRIGGLE, PH.D.
University Professor
School of Pharmacy and Pharmaceutical Sciences
State University of New York at Buffalo

CHELSEA HOUSE
PUBLISHERS
An imprint of Infobase Publishing

615.78
H447

LIBRARY
MILWAUKEE AREA TECHNICAL COLLEGE
Milwaukee Campus

WITHDRAWN

**Antidepressants and Antianxiety Drugs**

Copyright © 2011 by Infobase Publishing

All rights reserved. No part of this book may be reproduced or utilized in any form or by any means, electronic or mechanical, including photocopying, recording, or by any information storage or retrieval systems, without permission in writing from the publisher. For information, contact:

Chelsea House
An imprint of Infobase Publishing
132 West 31st Street
New York NY 10001

**Library of Congress Cataloging-in-Publication Data**

Hecht, Alan.
   Antidepressants and antianxiety drugs / Alan Hecht ; consulting editor, David J. Triggle.
      p.   cm.
   Includes bibliographical references and index.
   ISBN-13: 978-1-60413-532-9 (hardcover : alk. paper)
   ISBN-10: 1-60413-532-8 (hardcover : alk. paper)   1. Antidepressants.
   2. Tranquilizing drugs.   I. Triggle, D. J.   II. Title.

   RM332.H424 2010
   615′.78—dc22                                                    2010029224

Chelsea House books are available at special discounts when purchased in bulk quantities for businesses, associations, institutions, or sales promotions. Please call our Special Sales Department in New York at (212) 967-8800 or (800) 322-8755.

You can find Chelsea House on the World Wide Web at
http://www.chelseahouse.com

Text design by Kerry Casey
Cover design by Alicia Post
Composition by Newgen North America
Cover printed by Bang Printing, Brainerd, MN
Book printed and bound by Bang Printing, Brainerd, MN
Date printed: November 2010
Printed in the United States of America

10 9 8 7 6 5 4 3 2 1

This book is printed on acid-free paper.

All links and Web addresses were checked and verified to be correct at the time of publication. Because of the dynamic nature of the Web, some addresses and links may have changed since publication and may no longer be valid.

# Contents

# Foreword

## THE USE AND ABUSE OF DRUGS

For thousands of years, humans have used a variety of sources with which to cure their ills, cast out devils, promote their well-being, relieve their misery, and control their fertility. Until the beginning of the twentieth century, the agents used were all of natural origin, including many derived from plants as well as elements such as antimony, sulfur, mercury, and arsenic. The sixteenth-century alchemist and physician Paracelsus used mercury and arsenic in his treatment of syphilis, worms, and other diseases that were common at that time; his cure rates, however, remain unknown. Many drugs used today have their origins in natural products. Antimony derivatives, for example, are used in the treatment of the nasty tropical disease leishmaniasis. These plant-derived products represent molecules that have been "forged in the crucible of evolution" and continue to supply the scientist with molecular scaffolds for new drug development.

Our story of modern drug discovery may be considered to start with the German physician and scientist Paul Ehrlich, often called the father of chemotherapy. Born in 1854, Ehrlich became interested in the ways in which synthetic dyes, then becoming a major product of the German fine chemical industry, could selectively stain certain tissues and components of cells. He reasoned that such dyes might form the basis for drugs that could interact selectively with diseased or foreign cells and organisms. One of Ehrlich's early successes was development of the arsenical "606"—patented under the name *Salvarsan*—as a treatment for syphilis. Ehrlich's goal was to create a "magic bullet," a drug that would target only the diseased cell or the invading disease-causing organism and have no effect on healthy cells and tissues. In this he was not successful, but his great research did lay the groundwork for the successes of the twentieth century, including the discovery of the sulfonamides and the antibiotic penicillin. The latter agent saved countless lives during World War II. Ehrlich, like many scientists, was an optimist. On the eve of World War I, he wrote, "Now that the liability to, and danger of, disease are to a large extent circumscribed—the efforts of chemotherapeutics are directed as far as possible to fill up the gaps left in this ring." As we shall see in the pages of this volume, it is neither the first nor the last time that science has proclaimed its victory over nature, only to have to see this optimism dashed in the light of some freshly emerging infection.

From these advances, however, has come the vast array of drugs that are available to the modern physician. We are increasingly close to Ehrlich's magic bullet: Drugs can now target very specific molecular defects in a number of cancers, and doctors today have the ability to investigate the human genome to more effectively match the drug and the patient. In the next one to two decades, it is almost certain that the cost of "reading" an individual genome will be sufficiently cheap that, at least in the developed world, such personalized medicines will become the norm. The development of such drugs, however, is extremely costly and raises significant social issues, including equity in the delivery of medical treatment.

The twenty-first century will continue to produce major advances in medicines and medicine delivery. Nature is, however, a resilient foe. Diseases and organisms develop resistance to existing drugs, and new drugs must constantly be developed. (This is particularly true for anti-infective and anticancer agents.) Additionally, new and more lethal forms of existing infectious diseases can develop rapidly. With the ease of global travel, these can spread from Timbuktu to Toledo in less than 24 hours and become pandemics. Hence the current concerns with avian flu. Also, diseases that have previously been dormant or geographically circumscribed may suddenly break out worldwide. (Imagine, for example, a worldwide pandemic of Ebola disease, with public health agencies totally overwhelmed.) Finally, there are serious concerns regarding the possibility of man-made epidemics occurring through the deliberate or accidental spread of disease agents—including manufactured agents, such as smallpox with enhanced lethality. It is therefore imperative that the search for new medicines continue.

All of us at some time in our life will take a medicine, even if it is only aspirin for a headache or to reduce cosmetic defects. For some individuals, drug use will be constant throughout life. As we age, we will likely be exposed to a variety of medications—from childhood vaccines to drugs to relieve pain caused by a terminal disease. It is not easy to get accurate and understandable information about the drugs that we consume to treat diseases and disorders. There are, of course, highly specialized volumes aimed at medical or scientific professionals. These, however, demand a sophisticated knowledge base and experience to be comprehended. Advertising on television is widely available but provides only fleeting information, usually about only a single drug and designed to market rather than inform. The intent of this series of books, **Understanding Drugs**, is to provide the lay reader with intelligent, readable, and accurate descriptions of drugs, why and how they are used, their limitations, their side effects, and their future. The series will discuss both "treatment drugs"—typically, but not exclusively, prescription drugs, that have well-established criteria of both efficacy and safety—and "drugs of abuse," agents that have pronounced pharmacological and physiological effects but that are considered, for a variety of reasons, not to be considered for therapeutic purposes. It is our hope that these books will provide readers with sufficient information to satisfy their immediate needs and to serve as an adequate base for further investigation and for asking intelligent questions of health care providers.

—David J. Triggle, Ph.D.
University Professor
School of Pharmacy and Pharmaceutical Sciences
State University of New York at Buffalo

# 1

# Introduction: Antidepressants and Antianxiety Drugs

*Stephanie, a college freshman, just wasn't feeling right. For the past six months, she noticed that, at times, she felt anxious and tense. Her irritability level had increased and she found herself worrying about situations that would generally be insignificant to most other people. She was having difficulty sleeping and her mind was always "racing." Her thoughts often strayed to family matters, concerns about her health, and worries about her finances, although she really wasn't having any difficulties meeting her financial obligations. In addition, Stephanie found that her muscles always seemed to be achy, even when she wasn't exercising or overexerting herself.*

*Stephanie also noticed that she was tired all the time. Perhaps it was because her normal sleep patterns were disrupted. However, even if she did get a good night's sleep, she still felt exhausted in the morning. She was having difficulty focusing on her work in school and her assignments at home. Going out with her friends or her boyfriend just didn't seem to interest her anymore. She preferred to sit at home and stare at the television, sometimes not even remembering any details about what she just viewed.*

*She was not one to weigh herself often, but when she did, she noticed that she was losing weight. This was most likely due to Stephanie's loss of appetite and general disinterest in foods, even those she once enjoyed and went out of her way to eat. Nothing motivated her and she had a very bleak outlook on life in general. She always felt that her situation was dismal and had no possibility of improving. And what made it even worse was the constant feeling that she was going nowhere and that she was worthless. Stephanie was sure that she had no functional place in society.*

Stephanie is suffering from **generalized anxiety disorder (GAD)**, a condition that, in a majority of cases, is accompanied by **depression**.[1] In fact, most patients with **anxiety** also suffer from depression and vice versa.[2] GAD affects approximately 6.8 million Americans annually, with women affected in twice as many cases as men.[3] This statistic translates to approximately 3.1% of people age 18 or over in a given year. Overall, anxiety disorders are the most common mental illness in the United States, affecting 40 million adults.[4]

Millions of Americans suffer from depression and anxiety. Depression has been called "the common cold of mental illness." In the United States alone, depression costs more than $80 billion per year in medical costs and lost productivity. A study performed by the Kaiser Permanente health care organization showed that patients with anxiety and depression had 70% higher costs for their non-mental health general medical care than regular patients. Depression and anxiety affect one's general physical health and well-being.

More than 19 million people in the United States are suffering with anxiety disorders. However, less than one third of them are receiving proper treatment.[5] In addition, 43% of people with anxiety disorders also suffer with depression. As with depressive disorders, untreated anxiety disorders are associated with lower productivity at work and greater absenteeism, which end up costing approximately $42 billion annually.

Recent research has demonstrated that financial expenses are not the only costs associated with these conditions.[6] Researchers in London showed that anxious individuals often perform at the same level as non-anxious ones, but showed more effects of long-term stress. Anxious individuals read more slowly and took longer to solve a series of mathematical problems.

The cost of treating serious mental illness, which afflicts approximately 6% of American adults, is staggering. About $193.2 billion per year in lost earnings is the price tag associated with these conditions.[7] People suffering from serious mental illnesses, which include mood and anxiety disorders that seriously impair a person's ability to function for at least 30 days, earned at least 40% less than their peers who were in good mental health.

Anxiety and depression usually go hand in hand. It is often hard to separate them as distinct conditions as those who suffer with them frequently display symptoms of both at the same time.

# DEPRESSION

Depression is another common mental health condition that affects more than 1 in 20 Americans aged 12 and older.[8] This translates to 5.4% of all Americans in that age group. Interestingly, there is a predilection for the occurrence of depression in 40–59-year-olds, women, and non-Hispanic black people than in any other group. As one might expect, the rates for depression are higher in poor people as well.

The spectrum of symptoms associated with depression is broad and includes irritability, difficulty making decisions, crying for no apparent reason, loss of interest in normal, daily activities, loss of sex drive, changes in weight in both directions, difficulty sleeping, hopeless and sad feelings, and many additional problems.

Unfortunately, depression is often a cause for suicides. Those suffering from depression frequently have such poor feelings of self-worth that they contemplate suicide or, at the very least, imagine what it might be like to kill themselves. Without treatment, their situation often continues to spiral down so that they become virtually functionless and spend their days sitting around the house unable to become motivated about anything. This only makes them feel worse and increases their likelihood of suicide.

The causes of depression are many and varied. One factor is genetics. It has been observed that a family history of depression increases the risk of an individual developing the condition. Another factor is a serious illness. At times, depression can develop in response to a serious illness or may be caused by the presence of the illness.

One of the more obvious causes of depression is death of a loved one. At times, the death of a close relative or a friend does not even have to be a factor. If someone very close moves far away, this may trigger a depressive episode.

Loss of a job, getting divorced, or even positive events such as moving to a new home, getting a new job, or getting married may actually trigger depression in some people. It is the major change in their lives that causes the depression.

Another cause of depression that cannot be overlooked is substance abuse. Approximately 30% of individuals with substance abuse problems suffer from depression.[9] In some cases the abused drug itself is the cause of depression based on some biochemical change brought about by its presence in the body. In other instances the individual may be depressed because he or she is finding it extremely difficult to stop using the drug even though they truly want to.

Depression may also be found in women after giving birth. This type of depression, known as **post-partum depression**, is caused by the low hormone levels associated with having given birth. Right after delivery, the mother's estrogen and progesterone levels drop considerably. In many women this has a profound affect on their brain chemistry and may put them in a deep depression.

Sufferers of depression may find various forms of treatment such as medication, psychotherapy, and combinations of the two useful. Depending on the individual and the type and cause of depression, the psychiatrist or therapist will make a determination of exactly what course of treatment action to take.

As with anxiety disorders, those suffering with depression may find a number of support groups where help is available. Support is of the utmost importance if a person who is suffering has any hope of recovering, or at least learning to manage the condition.

## ANXIETY

Anxiety is also accompanied by both psychological and physical symptoms and complaints. Regardless of which of the many forms of anxiety a person is experiencing, he or she will have an unpleasant feeling accompanied by worry or fear. Often there is no obvious trigger that may be identified as causing an anxiety attack. In an individual who has no history of anxiety or panic attacks, anxiety may be considered a normal response to stress that allows the person to deal with a challenge.

There are several different causes for anxiety. As with many conditions and diseases, genetics often plays an important role. Several studies have suggested that a family history is strongly associated with the development of one or more anxiety conditions.[10]

Various forms of stress may also bring about an anxiety attack. These may be emotional stressors such as a divorce, death of a loved one, changing jobs or schools, moving to a new location, an upcoming wedding, or any number of others (as is the case with depression as well). Physiological triggers may include a serious illness, use of or withdrawal from addictive substances such as caffeine, nicotine, alcohol, and stronger recreational drugs, and other factors.

Anxiety can also be caused by an imbalance in brain **neurotransmitters**. Imbalances may be genetically based, brought about by abuse of drugs, naturally occurring, or may occur for reasons that are not clear. They interfere with the normal transmission of nerve impulses in the brain resulting in the misdirection or misinterpretation of messages traveling from one nerve to another. The brain then reacts differently to certain situations than it would under normal circumstances.

## ANTIDEPRESSANTS AND ANTIANXIETY DRUGS

Medications designed to treat anxiety and depression fall into the category of psychotherapeutic or psychotropic drugs. In general, they have made it possible for people with anxiety and depression to function on a daily basis and, in many cases, lead virtually normal lives without restrictions imposed upon them by their conditions.

Because each individual reacts to medications in his or her own way and because their response to medications may vary, pharmaceutical companies have developed many different drugs to treat anxiety and depression. These medications work in different ways and affect a variety of biochemical pathways and several areas of the brain.

Some people will experience an excellent response to a medication while others with the same condition might not respond at all or may find it necessary to use the same medication for a period of time much greater than those who responded quickly. Some conditions, such as schizophrenia, **bipolar disorder**, or long-standing depression or anxiety may require that a patient continues with medication for years.

Several factors may combine to determine how a medication will work in an individual. These include

- Type of mental disorder, such as depression, anxiety, bipolar disorder, and schizophrenia
- Age, sex, and body size
- Physical illnesses
- Habits like smoking and drinking
- Liver and kidney function
- Genetics
- Other medications and herbal/vitamin supplements
- Diet
- Whether medications are taken as prescribed.[11]

Because of these factors, it is impossible to predict to what degree a patient will have success when taking one or more medications for depression or anxiety thanks to these.

Antidepressants fall into the categories of **amphetamines** (Adderall, Ritalin), **monoamine oxidase inhibitors (MAOIs)** (Nardil, Parnate, Marplan), **tricyclic antidepressants (TCAs)** (Pamelor, Tofranil, Vivactil, Elavil), and, interestingly, many of the SSRIs and SNRIs that are discussed below.

Generally, the drugs prescribed to treat anxiety fall into the categories of **benzodiazepines** (Valium, Librium, Stelazine, Thorazine), **serotonin-norepinephrine reuptake inhibitors (SNRIs)** (Effexor, Cymbalta), **norepinephrine dopamine reuptake inhibitors (NDRIs)** and **selective serotonin reuptake inhibitors (SSRIs)** (Prozac, Zoloft, Paxil, Lexapro). As mentioned above, some of these may also be used to treat depression.

## Amphetamines

Amphetamines are classified as *psychostimulants*. These are drugs that bring about temporary improvements in physical functions, mental functions, or a combination of the two. The improvements may include an enhancement in wakefulness, alertness, and locomotion. This is one of the classes of drugs that is frequently used illicitly. The word is derived from the name of the basic chemical alpha-methylphenethylamine.

## Monoamine Oxidase Inhibitors (MAOIs)

As their name suggests, MAOIs inhibit the enzyme monoamine oxidase. This enzyme acts to break down neurotransmitters in the nervous system that are chemically classified as monoamines. This class includes dopamine, norepinephrine, epinephrine, histamine, serotonin, and several others. By inhibiting the enzyme and, thus the breakdown of the neurotransmitters, an increased number of nerve signals are able to be transmitted, causing a decrease in feelings of depression.

## Tricyclic Antidepressants (TCAs)

This class of antidepressants acts by inhibiting the reuptake transporters for serotonin and norepinephrine (acts as an SNRI). This makes more of these neurotransmitters available at the synapses in the brain, leading to an increase in nerve impulse transmissions. The increased transmissions change behavior and help to relieve depression. Because TCAs are associated with a large number of side effects, they are no longer used extensively and have been replaced by safer SSRIs and SNRIs (discussed below).

## Benzodiazepines

These drugs act to enhance the action of the neurotransmitter gamma amino butyric acid (GABA), an inhibitory neurotransmitter that creates a sedative and hypnotic effect and is able to act as a muscle relaxant and anticonvulsant. Generally, they are safe to use for short periods of time, but long-term use often leads to addiction. In addition, a relapse of the anxiety upon discontinuation of the drugs is not uncommon.

## Serotonin-Norepinephrine Reuptake Inhibitors (SNRIs)

Although generally used to treat depression, these drugs are also prescribed to treat anxiety in many cases. They act by blocking the transporters that bring the neurotransmitters serotonin and norepinephrine from the synapses back into the nerve endings. By allowing the neurotransmitters to remain in the synapses for a longer time, more impulses are transmitted and behavior is modified to quell anxiety. They appear to have a greater antianxiety efficacy and fewer side effects than SSRIs.

## Norepinephrine Dopamine Reuptake Inhibitors (NDRIs)

This class of drugs acts to inhibit the reuptake of both the neurotransmitters norepinephrine and dopamine by blocking their reuptake transporters in a fashion similar to that of SNRIs. The result is an increase in the available amount of both norepinephrine and dopamine in the synapses of the brain. This leads to a decrease in symptoms of depression such as irritability and sadness. The two most frequently prescribed members of this class of drugs are bupropion (Wellbutrin) and methylphenidate (Ritalin).

## Selective Serotonin Reuptake Inhibitors (SSRIs)

These drugs work in the same way as SNRIs, but they only block serotonin reuptake transporters, which is why they are referred to as selective. The result of their actions is an increase in the level of the neurotransmitter serotonin being available in the synapses to help transmit more impulses in the brain. Once again, behavior is modified and anxiety is reduced.

# 2

# History of Antidepressants and Antianxiety Drugs

*The year was 1955 and Fred was beginning to find that he was feeling increasingly tense and irritable. He was having difficulty sleeping at night, had trouble concentrating at work, felt a relative mild tightness in his chest, was short-tempered with coworkers and family members, and felt like he was on "pins and needles" all the time.*

*One afternoon while at his job, Fred began to feel more tightness in his chest and he became light-headed. His face began to turn red and he experienced shortness of breath. His boss immediately called for an ambulance and he was taken to a local hospital.*

*After a thorough examination, it was determined that Fred was not having a heart attack, as he initially thought, but was suffering from an extreme anxiety attack due to stress and overwork. The hospital doctors immediately gave him Miltown (meprobamate), a new drug to treat anxiety. Within minutes he began to feel considerably better.*

*Fred was advised to visit his family doctor for follow-up care and to receive a prescription for continued treatment with Miltown.*

Numerous antidepressants and antianxiety agents have been developed over a period of many years. This historical development has yielded a variety of drugs in several different categories, all of which are aimed at the successful treatment of depression and anxiety. Of course, each person may react differently to a particular drug. Thus, pharmaceutical companies have been forced to continually come up with new drugs that will work in individuals who don't respond to other available medications.

The use of drugs to treat mental disorders can be traced back to the late 19th century when **lithium** was used to treat inmates of insane asylums.[1] The causes of the various illnesses as well as the mechanism of action of the lithium were poorly understood.

# ANTIDEPRESSANTS

In the early 20th century, common treatments for depression included opiates (drugs derived from the dried, condensed juice of the poppy *Papaver somniferum*) and amphetamines (central nervous system stimulants that counteract depression and control appetite). The problem with these medications was that they were addictive, and this made them much less desirable as newer medications were developed.

In 1951 the antituberculosis drugs iproniazid and isoniazid, being tested by doctors Irving Selikoff and Edward Robitzek, were found to act as an antidepressant when administered to patients with the disease.[2] The patients became less depressed, more optimistic, and more active. A year later, psychiatrists Max Lurie and Harry Salzer used isoniazid to treat depressed patients and found that two thirds of their patients improved.[3]

In 1957 researchers found that these drugs slowed the enzymatic breakdown of the neurotransmitters dopamine, norepinephrine, and serotonin. They did this by interfering with the enzyme monoamine oxidase. Thus, this class of medications became known as monoamine oxidase inhibitors (MAOIs). The drugs were not put into extensive use, however, for about 10 years.[4] The reason was that use of the original MAOIs was accompanied by serious side effects that reduced their popularity. When forms of these drugs that inhibited only the monoamine oxidase A subtype were developed, the number and severity of side effects was greatly diminished and the MAOIs became more widely used.

Researchers continued to work on other categories of antidepressants and developed a group called tricyclic antidepressants (TCAs). This class of drugs began to be widely used by 1955. The first TCA used was chlorpromazine (Thorazine), which was synthesized in 1950. It was originally used as an antipsychotic medication. Imipramine (Tofranil) was created in 1955 and put on the market in 1957. Following this, amitriptyline (Elavil) was created and was introduced in 1961.

TCAs were created by modifying a group of drugs known as phenothia-zines, which were first used as insecticides in 1935. TCAs blocked the removal of the neurotransmitters norepinephrine and serotonin from the synapses in

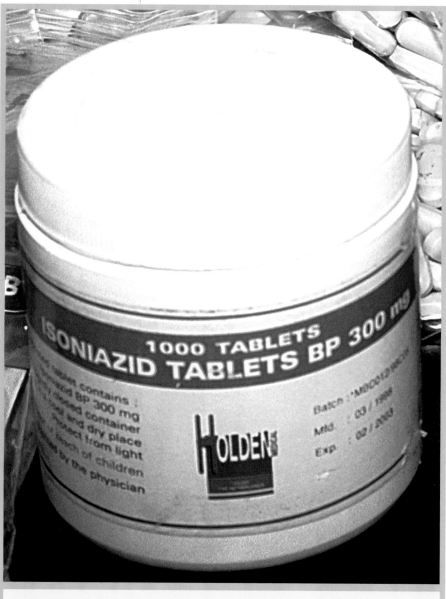

**Figure 2.1  Isoniazid.**  (*© Photo Researchers Inc.*)

the brain. This removal process is called reuptake and will be discussed in detail in chapter 4.

Both MAOIs and TCAs were a definite improvement in the treatments available for depression, but early versions had serious toxicity and safety issues and could cause heavy sedation and drug interactions. Additional modifications yielded the development of safer TCAs like amitriptyline and desipramine.

In addition to continued drug research, scientists began to learn more about how the nervous system functions and how the various drugs used to treat depression actually worked on the nervous system. This helped researchers to better understand the causes of different mental illnesses and which drugs would work best to treat them. There was, however, disagreement as to what caused depression.

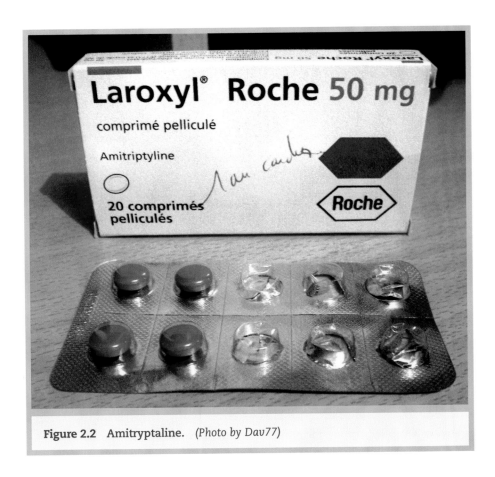

**Figure 2.2   Amitryptaline.**   *(Photo by Dav77)*

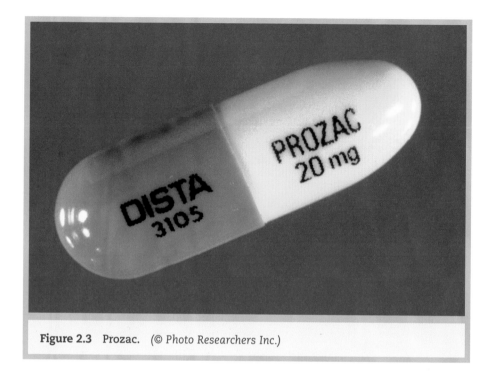

**Figure 2.3** **Prozac.** *(© Photo Researchers Inc.)*

Some scientists believed that decreases in the neurotransmitter norepinephrine led to depression while others were certain that it was deficits in the neurotransmitter serotonin that were responsible. Those who agreed with the latter began to work with the antihistamine diphenhydramine (Benadryl) and were able to modify it to create fluoxetine (Prozac) in 1987, which was the first selective serotonin reuptake inhibitor (SSRI).[5] It was first administered and its actions studied by Dr. Louis Lemberger, however, Bryan Molloy and Robert Rathbun began the work that eventually led to its discovery at the Eli Lilly pharmaceutical company in 1970. SSRIs were shown to be very effective in treating depression with significantly reduced side effects, and they became the most widely prescribed antidepressants.

Since there was uncertainty as to which neurotransmitter was involved in causing depression—serotonin or norepinephrine—another group of antidepressants was created in the 1990s. These were the serotonin-norepinephrine reuptake inhibitors (SNRIs). They affect both neurotransmitters, once again by inhibiting their reuptake into the nerves that release them in the

# TIMELINE OF THE DEVELOPMENT OF ANTIDEPRESSANT DRUGS

**Early 1900s:** Coining of term *psychopharmacology;* use of electroconvulsive therapy for depression initiated; minimally successful attempt to treat depression pharmacologically.

**1950s:** Development of phenothiazines; synthesis and clinical use of clorpromazine for psychosis; discovery of iproniazid's (and MAOIs') antidepressant effects in tuberculosis patients; synthesis of other MAOIs like tranylcypromine; synthesis and beginning use of TCAs, like imipramine, for depression.

**1960s:** Beginnings of broad clinical use of TCAs, like amitriptyline, now preferred over MAOIs; catecholamine hypothesis of depression now widely discussed and investigated.

**1970–1990s:** Development and clinical use of SSRIs like fluoxetine, citalopram, and sertraline; broadening use of antidepressants for other conditions like anxiety disorders and painful circumstances; more common prescribing of antidepressant agents by primary care physicians.

**1990–early 2000s:** Synthesis and clinical use of dual-acting (NE and 5-HT) antidepressants, with fewer TCA-like side effects, including SNRIs (venlafaxine, duloxetine) mirtazapine, bupropion, and nefazodone; more rigorous investigation of the analgesic properties of newer antidepressant agents.

Source: Joseph A. Lieberman, MD. "History of the Use of Antidepressants in Primary Care," *Primary Care Companion Journal of Clinical Psychiatry* 5, suppl. 7 (2003): 6–10.

brain. They are designed to treat major depression as well as anxiety disorders, obsessive-compulsive disorder, attention-deficit/hyperactivity disorder (ADHD), and a few other conditions. The most widely used today are venlafaxine (Effexor), duloxetine (Cymbalta), and desvenlafaxine (Pristiq).

Anxiety and depression often go hand in hand. With this in mind, some physicians discovered that MAOIs and TCAs, although generally used for the treatment of depression, were also effective against anxiety and the relief of chronic pain. In addition, SSRIs were also found to be useful in treating patients with anxiety.[6]

## ANTIANXIETY DRUGS

Probably the first antianxiety drug used was barbital, a barbiturate synthesized by Emil Fischer and Joseph von Mering in Germany in 1903. They found that it was effective in putting dogs to sleep and marketed the drug under the brand name Veronal. Its precursor, barbituric acid, was first synthesized by Adolph von Baeyer in 1864 in Germany by condensing urea from animal urine with diethyl malonate that came from apples. It had no medical value at the time. However, since its discovery, more than 2500 compounds with pharmacologically active properties have been synthesized. Those most commonly used are phenobarbital, pentobarbital, and secobarbital. Because of the high risk of addiction and death due to overdoses, benzodiazepines

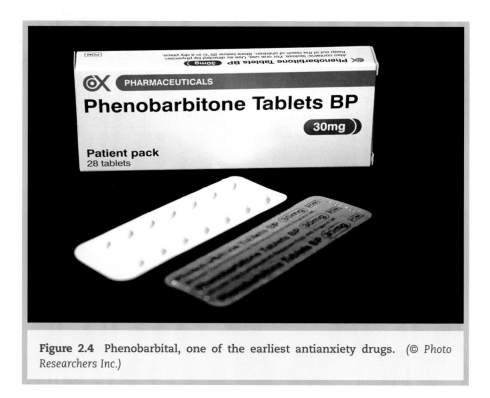

**Figure 2.4** Phenobarbital, one of the earliest antianxiety drugs. (© *Photo Researchers Inc.*)

## TIMELINE OF THE DEVELOPMENT OF MORE WIDELY PRESCRIBED ANTIANXIETY DRUGS

**1959:** Chlordiazepoxide (Librium)

**1962:** Oxazepam (Serax)

**1963:** Diazepam (Valium)

**1975:** Clonazepam (Klonopin)

**1976:** Alprazolam (Xanax)

**1977:** Lorazepam (Ativan)

**1994:** Zolpidem (Ambien)

**2005:** Eszopiclone (Lunesta)

have largely replaced barbiturates in treating anxiety as they have a smaller potential for lethal overdoses.

Probably the most famous and widely used antianxiety agent (anxiolytic), also referred to as a tranquilizer, was manufactured in 1955 in Milltown, New Jersey. The pill was named for this small village and was called Miltown. Meprobamate was first synthesized by Bernard John Ludwig and Frank Milan Berger, MD at Carter Products in May 1950.

Dr. Berger was working in the 1940s to find a preservative for penicillin. He noticed that the chemical he was testing had a tranquilizing effect on the small animals he was using for his research. He moved from his laboratory in Great Britain to Wallace Laboratories, a pharmaceutical company in New Jersey where he met Bernard Ludwig, a chemist. Together they synthesized meprobamate and named it Miltown. Dr. Berger referred to Miltown as a relaxant of the central nervous system whereas other drugs acted to suppress it.

In 1955, a study was performed on 101 patients confined to Mississippi State Hospital in Whitfield, Mississippi. The patients had what was referred to as "mental symptoms." The overall success rate in helping to alleviate symptoms in a majority of the patients helped to put Miltown in the forefront of the medicinal world. In 1956, doctors were prescribing it to treat alcoholism. By

**Figure 2.5** Valium, the most prescribed drug between 1969 and 1982. *(Drug Enforcement Administration)*

1957, more than 36 million prescriptions had been filled in the United States with even more filled worldwide. In fact, approximately one third of all prescriptions written were for Miltown.[7]

Meprobamate's popularity decreased over the years and by 1970 it was discovered to be addictive. It was replaced by drugs in the class known as benzodiazepines, which were actually discovered ten years earlier by Dr. Leo Sternbach. The first of these drugs was Librium, generically known as chlordiazepoxide. Shortly after its appearance, another benzodiazepine, Valium, generically known as diazepam, became popular. In fact, Valium's popularity was so great that it became the most prescribed drug in America between 1969 and 1982.

The benzodiazepines were a definite improvement over meprobamate, but it was discovered that with long-term use they can become addictive, cause physical dependence, and if not slowly tapered, will lead to serious withdrawal symptoms when therapy stops in a patient who has developed dependence. This benzodiazepine withdrawal syndrome is accompanied by many symptoms. Some of the most common and serious are nightmares, **insomnia**, agitation, anxiety, panic attacks, headaches, aches and pains, impaired memory and concentration, confusion, and psychosis.[8]

The timeline on page 23 shows the development of the most widely used benzodiazepines as well as some non-benzodiazepines that have come into use as a replacement for them. The inherent problems associated with the use of the benzodiazepines have given drug manufacturers the incentive to create other drugs to treat the same conditions without the serious side affects.

Librium was developed as a sedative/hypnotic drug to treat anxiety and muscle spasms. Within a few years, Valium became available and became the drug of choice to treat what Librium had been used for because it was better tolerated. During this same time period, Serax was developed to treat the same conditions as the other two medications and, additionally, for those patients with bipolar disorder. This condition causes patient to have periods of serious depression alternating with feelings of euphoria. The degrees vary from patient to patient and even within the patient.

Klonopin was developed also as an antianxiety agent, but had an additional benefit in that it could be used as an anticonvulsant in epileptics. Xanax was created as an anxiolytic, anticonvulsant, and to treat panic attacks. Ativan has a similar range of treatments as the other benzodiazepines, but is unique in that it may be used as an antiemetic. Antiemetics are drugs that inhibit vomiting and, as such, are useful in patients receiving cancer chemotherapy, which is often associated with severe, recurrent vomiting.

Ambien was created 15 years after the benzodiazepines and is similar in its actions, but is chemically different from them. It is used specifically to treat insomnia. It is in the imidazopyridine class of drugs. Lunesta, also used to treat insomnia, appears to be safer than Ambien and is able to be used by the elderly and younger adults. It is in a class of drugs known as cyclopyrrolones.

# 3
# Causes and Consequences of Depression and Anxiety

*Mike, a Marine corporal, had been stationed in the Iraqi province of Al Anbar during the height of the Iraq War. He was often under fire from enemy forces using rocket-propelled grenades, mortars, missiles, car bombs, and various other guerilla tactics. His days were always filled with very loud explosive noises, the whistling sound of incoming ammunition, and the constant concern that death was not far away.*

*When Mike's tour of duty was over and he returned to his home in Michigan, he was not the same person that everybody knew when he left to serve. He was more tense, he always felt that something bad was going to happen, his overall attitude was negative, and he would react violently to loud sounds and whistling noises. One day, while walking down the main street of his small town, a car backfired. Mike immediately dove under a parked car yelling, "Hit the dirt!" Of course, after a few seconds he realized that there was no danger and he slowly crawled out from under the car feeling very embarrassed at what he had done.*

## DEPRESSION

There are many different triggers for depression including divorce, death of a loved one, and loss of a job. Although there are many events that may trigger depression, the actual biological causes are at the heart of a depressive episode. A particular occurrence may cause depression in one individual and only temporary sadness in another. This is where biology becomes involved.

There are more than 30 different neurotransmitters in the brain, but three of them appear to be most directly related to clinical depression. They are serotonin, norepinephrine, and dopamine. They appear to be most closely associated with appetite, sexuality, sleep, reactions to stress, and regulating emotions.

Much of what has been learned about how these neurotransmitters work in the brain has developed as a result of observing responses to various medications that affect depression. It is clear that the SSRIs, SNRIs, TCAs, NDRIs, and others have a direct affect on the amount of neurotransmitters in the synapses. However, the exact mechanism used by these neurotransmitters to bring about behavioral changes is not clear.

For example, it is known that some people suffering from clinical depression have low levels of norepinephrine (NE). Using SNRIs to ensure that more NE remains in the synapses of the brain has been shown to relieve many cases of clinical depression. However, there are also some cases of clinical depression that are associated with higher than normal levels of NE.

Another confusing aspect of the relationship between neurotransmitters and clinical depression is the fact that specific antidepressants don't work for everyone. Because each of us is an individual with slightly different biochemistries, what works well in one person may not work at all in another. Basically, we know that there is a relationship between neurotransmitters and clinical depression, but exactly what that relationship is remains unclear. We are not sure if changes in neurotransmitters cause depression or if depression causes changes in neurotransmitters. One fact is accepted by all researchers, and that is that no single cause gives rise to depression.

In searching for answers as to the causes of depression, recent research has shown that even enzymes may be responsible. In a study involving mice given a vaccine for tuberculosis, the stimulation of their immune systems led to depressive-like symptoms. The enzyme indoleamine 2,3-dioxygenase (IDO) is activated by chemicals called cytokines that are released by cells of the immune system when it is challenged by viruses or bacteria. In these mice, if the enzyme was blocked, no depressive symptoms developed. At this time, the exact mechanism for the development of depression by IDO is not known, but further work is being done to better understand the mechanism.[1]

# HOW DEPRESSION AFFECTS THE BODY

Depression is often associated with the development of several physical consequences. In addition to the obvious increased risk for suicide, depressed individuals are four times more likely to suffer a heart attack.[2] In addition, if the symptoms of depression persist after the heart attack, the prognosis is worse.

Another physical finding is restricted to women. It appears that women suffering with depression have reduced bone mineral density and are more prone to hip fractures in their later years than women who have never suffered from it.

The apparent cause of these physical manifestations of depression is the activation of the body's main stress system. Depressed people have elevated levels of the hormone **cortisol**, which is associated with decreased bone mineral density and the redistribution of body fat that might lead to an increased risk of heart disease. In one study, intra-abdominal fat content was twice as high in depressive females than in healthy ones.[3] This is known to be a factor in the increased risk of heart disease. In addition, these individuals developed an alteration in their platelets, the cell fragments in blood that are involved in the clotting process. This increased the risk of forming blood clots, which also increases the risk for a heart attack.

Other physical problems associated with depression include diabetes, a greater susceptibility to catching human immunodeficiency virus (HIV) and developing acquired immunodeficiency syndrome (AIDS), strokes, and a poorer prognosis when suffering with cancer.[4]

# HOW DEPRESSION AFFECTS LIFESTYLES

Aside from health risks, depression is associated with several other consequences including financial hardships. One very interesting study showed that financial hardships in depressed Floridians were 75% higher than the national average. Self-reported credit card debt and the negative social consequences caused by depression contributed more than $19,400 in out-of-pocket costs for Floridians. This was approximately $8,300 more than other Americans living with depression.[5]

In addition to the financial burden brought about by depression, the study also revealed that only one half of the people participating in the research were satisfied with their marital relationships. This is only one of the social impacts of depression. Job prospects are also affected when an individual is depressed. Functioning at work is seriously affected by depression and may lead to demotions and loss of jobs altogether.

Studies have been done to determine what sociological factors might contribute to the development of depression. In Australia, a National Depression Index was created to determine which groups would be at an elevated risk of developing depression. It was determined that both income level and employment status had a bearing on the incidence of depression in society.[6]

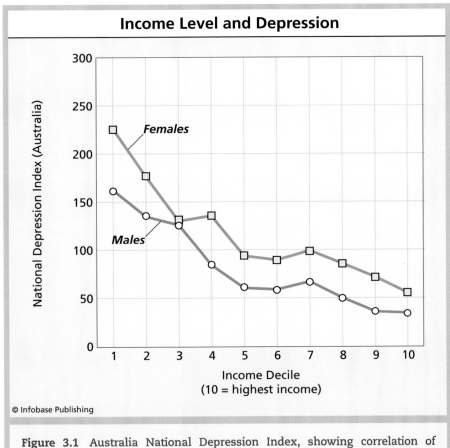

Figure 3.1 Australia National Depression Index, showing correlation of income level and depression.

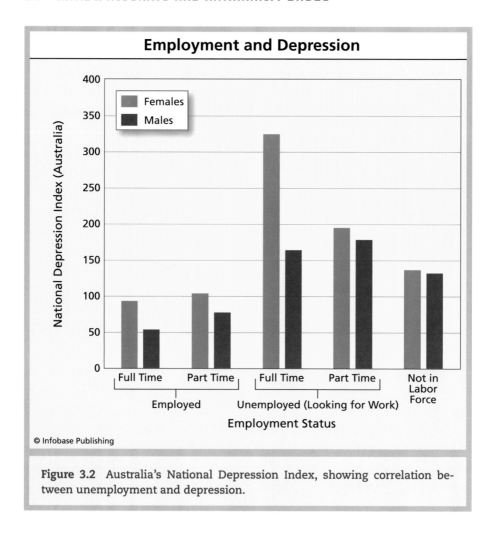

**Figure 3.2** Australia's National Depression Index, showing correlation between unemployment and depression.

# ANXIETY

As with depression, the biological causes of anxiety are not clear. Scientists and researchers agree that the most likely causes are personality (which has a genetic basis), heredity, brain chemistry, and life experiences.

People with a personality that manifests as poor coping skills and low self-esteem are more prone to anxiety attacks. The reason behind this is not clear, but it is accepted simply by analyzing the statistics.

Studies involving identical twins have shown that anxiety attacks occur more frequently in the second twin if the first has anxiety attacks. When non-identical twins are compared, the occurrence in the first twin has no bearing on the incidence in the second.

Women have a higher incidence of anxiety disorders than men. This has been attributed to the presence of female hormones that are not in men. It has been suggested that the female hormones, particularly progesterone, affect the neurotransmitters in the brain leading to anxiety attacks. However, the exact mechanism is unknown.

From a biochemical standpoint, an imbalance in the levels of various neurotransmitters in the brain often leads to anxiety attacks. This, in combination with a stress-filled lifestyle, traumatic events, or some unknown causes, will often lead to the development of anxiety.

Of course, anxiety also has a number of symptoms associated with it as well as consequences beyond physical affects. Physically, individuals suffering with anxiety often feel muscle tension and aches, sweaty or clammy palms, elevated heart rate, tiredness from difficulty sleeping, a feeling of fullness in the throat (*globus hystericus*), trembling, shaking or twitching, and even occasional dizziness.

Emotionally, anxiety sufferers experience difficulty concentrating, feelings of dread and doom, irritability and restlessness associated with feeling on edge all the time, excessive worry, and always expecting something bad is going to happen.

Socially, anxiety may have severe consequences on a person's life. Being anxious may cause an adult to avoid interacting with other people while at work or in social situations. Naturally, this may have an affect on the individual's ability to perform his or her job successfully as interactions with coworkers are often necessary for successful completion of work responsibilities. Anxiety in children may also cause them to avoid making new friends or even socializing with already established ones, thus leading to little interaction outside of the family.

In both adults and children, anxiety may lead to the development of physical symptoms such as headaches and stomach aches that cause the individual to miss work or school. Once again, this may have serious consequences on maintaining a position of employment or completing the school year successfully.

Various forms of anxiety are quite pervasive in society. Figure 3.3 provides an informative comparison of several types of anxiety and their relative incidence among adults in the United States.

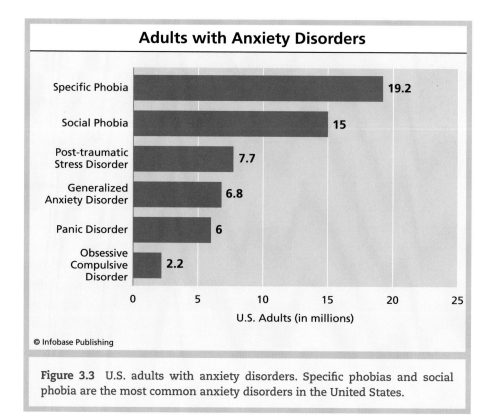

**Figure 3.3** U.S. adults with anxiety disorders. Specific phobias and social phobia are the most common anxiety disorders in the United States.

When considering all of the statistics and research findings, it is clear that depression and anxiety occur in a fairly sizeable percentage of the population and have far-reaching effects in many areas of everyday life. Successful treatment of these conditions is crucial in aiding not only the individuals suffering with them, but society as a whole.

## POST-TRAUMATIC STRESS DISORDER (PTSD)

What happened to Mike has happened to many returning military personnel after their tours of duty were over or the wars had ended. During World War II, this response was known as "shell shock." Today we know it as post-traumatic stress disorder (PTSD), a condition that may develop following a seriously traumatic or life-threatening incident in a person's life.

According to the National Center for PTSD of the U.S. Department of Veterans Affairs, there are several events that may lead to PTSD.[7] These include

- Combat or military exposure
- Child sexual or physical abuse
- Terrorist attacks
- Sexual or physical assault
- Serious accidents, such as a car wreck
- Natural disasters, such as a fire, tornado, hurricane, flood, or earthquake

PTSD is considered an anxiety disorder and is associated with specific behaviors that indicate a condition very different from the normal emotional response that the average individual experiences following a traumatic event. In such cases, the person responds to the stressor with less intensity and recovers in a reasonable period of time. In cases of PTSD, the person reacts with excessive intensity and may never recover.

To diagnose this condition, the doctor must observe several different signs that the patient may present. These include a state of increased arousal such as insomnia, difficulty staying asleep, anger, avoidance of specific stimuli associated with the original trauma, and nightmares and flashbacks relating to the trauma. The clinical picture must last for more than six months and cause the patient significant occupational and/or social impairment, which would include problems at work or in relationships with other people.[8]

PTSD became a household term following the events of September 11, 2001, and also when discussing soldiers returning from the Gulf, Iraq, and Afghanistan Wars. The condition may occur immediately or not show up for weeks or months after the traumatic event.

PTSD is an anxiety disorder that affects some individuals following their observation or actual experience of a dangerous or life-threatening event. Although the body is "hard-wired" to respond to such events with the **fight-or-flight response** in order to survive such events, in cases of PTSD the response continues long after the danger is over. The actual response is based on an elevation in levels of epinephrine (adrenaline) and, to a lesser degree norepinephrine, hormones that bring about several changes in the body.

These hormones are secreted by the medulla (central portion) of the adrenal glands.

To deal directly with a threat or to be able to escape unharmed, several physiological changes take place in a fraction of a second. These include an elevation in heart and respiratory rates designed to bring in more oxygen and pump more blood to the muscles of the body so that fighting or fleeing may take place more easily. The pupils dilate to allow the eyes to get a better view of the impending danger. Blood vessels to the skeletal muscles dilate to increase the supply of nutrients and oxygen to these muscles so that they may function to their maximum capacity. At the same time, blood vessels supplying many of the organs, except the heart, will constrict so that the blood may be redirected to the muscles. At this point, there is no need for the body to concentrate on digesting food, for example.

Once the danger has passed, the secretion of the two hormones subsides and levels return to their previous state. Unfortunately, those suffering with PTSD continue to feel frightened and stressed even when the danger has passed. The condition may strike anyone at any age. It is more commonly seen in war veterans, survivors of a catastrophic event such as the World Trade Center disaster, victims of accidents, sexual abuse, earthquakes, and any other threatening event.

This form of anxiety presents its symptoms in one of three categories. The first is re-experiencing symptoms. Here, the individual can have bad dreams, frightening thoughts, and/or flashbacks, which are the repeated reliving of the particular trauma that caused the PTSD. During a flashback, the person will also experience the physical symptoms that occurred during the trauma such as sweating, rapid breathing, rapid heart rate, and any other responses that originally took place.

The second category is avoidance symptoms. Here, the individual will utilize various means to avoid any memory of the trauma. For example, he or she may actually have trouble remembering the event. This is a defense mechanism that the mind will utilize to calm itself down. Another technique is to avoid places, objects, or events that remind the individual of the traumatic experience. The person might lose interest in activities that were once enjoyable because something might trigger a memory of the traumatic experience. Sometimes, complete emotional numbness might be experienced. This will help the individual to avoid the negative feelings associated with the trauma

# PTSD: FACTORS AFFECTING ITS OCCURRENCE

Although many people have experienced traumatic events, only some actually develop PTSD. The obvious question is, why? Several factors will help a person avoid the development of PTSD while other factors will lead to it. The National Institute of Mental Health has summarized these factors to help explain how this happens.
Risk factors for PTSD include

- Living through dangerous events and traumas
- Having a history of mental illness
- Getting hurt
- Seeing people hurt or killed
- Feeling horror, helplessness, or extreme fear
- Having little or no social support after the event
- Dealing with extra stress after the event, such as loss of a loved one, pain and injury, or loss of a job or home

Resilience factors that may reduce the risk of PTSD include

- Seeking out support from other people, such as friends and family
- Finding a support group after a traumatic event
- Feeling good about one's own actions in the face of danger
- Having a coping strategy, or a way of getting through the bad event and learning from it
- Being able to act and respond effectively despite feeling fear

National Institute of Mental Health, "Post-Traumatic Stress Disorder (PTSD)," http://www.nimh.nih.gov/health/publications/post-traumatic-stress-disorder-ptsd/nimh_ptsd_booklet.pdf.

and keep him or her from experiencing the physiological responses associated with it.

The third category of symptoms is hyperarousal. Here, the individual always feels tense and edgy. He or she will startle easily, have difficulty sleeping, and frequently display angry outbursts. Unfortunately, these symptoms tend to be present all of the time rather than being triggered by a specific event or memory. This constant presence makes everyday living very difficult as most activities are disrupted by the symptoms.

The symptoms of PTSD may be very different in children than they are in adults. Younger children will frequently become very clingy to a parent or other adult, sometimes forget how to speak, begin to wet the bed even though they were already trained, and act out the scary event during play. Teens and older children will often react in the same ways as adults do. However, they may also develop destructive, disruptive, or disrespectful behaviors.

## GENES AND BIOCHEMISTRY

Clearly, there is no question as to the precipitating factor that caused Mike's anxiety in the case history at the beginning of this chapter. However, the actual reason for why Mike responded the way he did while other military personnel in the same area were able to come home and lead a normal life is not clear.

Since the ways in which the brain functions are based strongly on biochemistry, it is not surprising that a biochemical imbalance in the brain might lead to anxiety disorders. These imbalances may be isolated to the individual or may be the result of a genetically inherited biochemical imbalance that appears in other family members.

A study performed by Finnish scientists has shown that there is a genetic predisposition to developing anxiety. The study even showed that there are specific genes associated with different types of anxiety such as panic disorder, generalized anxiety disorder, and social phobias.[9] Various environmental occurrences, such as a traumatic event, have a greater probability of triggering an anxiety attack in genetically predisposed individuals. In addition, there is a greater probability of developing anxiety disorders in identical twins if one twin already is suffering. And it has been shown that children of parents with panic disorder have an eight times greater chance of developing the same condition.[10]

## PERSONALITY

It is also possible that personality has a strong impact on the development of anxiety disorders. It has been proposed that there is a cyclic reinforcement of the development of psychiatric disorders in patients with low self-esteem.[11] That is, low self-esteem can lead to the development of these disorders. Suffering from these disorders causes the patient to develop an even lower self-esteem. This brings about a worsening of the psychiatric condition that lowers self-esteem even more.

One other area studied points to life experiences as a cause of anxiety disorders. A traumatic event may be a trigger for specific phobias, PTSD, or acute stress disorder.[12] The two stress disorders begin within days of the precipitating experience. Phobias may take some time to develop, but with careful and thorough investigation, may be traced back to the experience. In addition, some people who suffer from anxiety disorders have never experienced a particularly stressful event.

## GENERALIZED ANXIETY DISORDER

Generalized anxiety disorder (GAD) is manifested as excessive, amplified anxiety and worry about common events that occur almost every day. People with this disorder are always expecting some disaster to take place. They tend to worry excessively about their health, finances, their families, work, school, and anything else they can focus on. These worries are unrealistic because they are not based on any truly serious situations that would cause anxiety in an individual who is not suffering from GAD.

These individuals struggle to get through each day because their fears and concerns are so out of proportion to reality that they find it difficult to function at home, in school, at work, and in society in general. Their relationships with other family members, friends, colleagues at work, fellow students, and people in general suffer severely. If untreated, the effects can be devastating as relationships crumble, jobs are lost, and school courses are failed.

Physiologically, GAD presents with a variety of symptoms affecting several systems of the body. It is not unusual for an individual to suffer with headaches, muscle tension, tiredness, irritability, difficulty concentrating, sweating, frequent visits to the bathroom to urinate, indigestion, difficulty falling asleep and staying asleep, and several other complaints relating to various systems of the body.

GAD is a condition that takes time to develop. Frequently, it begins at some point between childhood and middle age, which means it's difficult to predict when it will strike most people. Once a person is suffering with it, the symptoms will vary in intensity getting better or worse in relation to what is going on in his or her life. As one would expect, symptoms become worse during times of stress.

A definitive diagnosis of GAD is not often made on the first visit to the doctor's office. The patient will usually visit looking for relief from specific complaints such as headaches, difficulty sleeping, irritability, or some other discomfort. When the treatment provided doesn't eliminate the problem, further studies become necessary. Eventually, the diagnosis of GAD is usually made and proper treatment may begin. This may not occur until the family doctor refers the patient to a mental health specialist.

Medications used to treat GAD vary and many factors are taken into consideration by the treating physician when prescribing treatment. In some cases, the obvious treatment is with antianxiety medications. Other patients may respond better to antidepressants. Some doctors prescribe a class of medications called beta blockers that work differently from the medicines mentioned above. A detailed explanation of the different categories of drugs used and medications within these categories will be covered in chapter 4.

In addition to medical treatments, many patients will undergo psychotherapy with a psychiatrist, psychologist, or clinical social worker. In most cases, these patients will continue to take prescribed medications while receiving the psychotherapy. This combination is often much more effective than either mode of treatment alone.

## SOCIAL PHOBIA

Another form of anxiety that affects people is social phobia (also known as social anxiety). This condition is associated with fears that other people are judging the individual and fears of being embarrassed. It is true that almost everybody, at one time or another, has been concerned about looking foolish in front of their peers or strangers. This is a normal emotion. However, people with social phobia take this fear to the extreme and it interferes with their lives on a daily basis. Everyday functions are difficult to perform and the individual's entire relationship with society suffers.

People with this condition are afraid of performing simple tasks in front of others. Some of these might include eating or drinking in public, answering questions in class, making eye contact with peers, attending a meeting at work, making a phone call, fear of meeting new people, inability to sign a check in front of a cashier, and numerous others. Some of these events may cause the individual to worry about them for weeks in advance.

Although people with social phobia realize that their fears are excessive and unwarranted, they can't help themselves. They often practice avoidance behaviors so that they aren't exposed to the fear-causing event. These behaviors may go as far as avoiding particular people, staying away from places where an event might occur, and even staying at home rather than venturing out into the world. This seriously interferes with their daily functions.

Symptoms associated with social phobia are often very similar from one sufferer to another. They are typical of a person who is feeling abject fear. They include heavy sweating, nausea, trembling, blushing, difficulty speaking, rapid heart rate, and rapid breathing (sometimes actually hyperventilating). Some individuals will use alcohol to help them get through situations that they cannot avoid. This may lead to alcoholism and behaviors that make the situation worse. Drugs used to treat this condition will be discussed in chapter 4.

This condition often begins in childhood or teen years around puberty. It may last for only a few years and then subside, or it may last a lifetime. Some factors that determine whether a person develops social phobia are a family history, a negative humiliating triggering event in the person's life such as having to speak publicly, problems in developing social skills leading to the development of the phobia, and imbalances in brain neurotransmitters, particularly serotonin and any of several other causes.

## OBSESSIVE-COMPULSIVE DISORDER (OCD)

Another condition included in the broad spectrum of anxiety is obsessive-compulsive disorder (OCD). This disorder is characterized by persistent, disruptive, upsetting thoughts (the obsession), and ritualistic repetitive actions (the compulsion). The compulsions occur as an attempt to control the anxiety brought about by the obsessive thoughts.

Depending on the obsession, the compulsion may take any number of forms. For example, an individual who is overly concerned with the safety of his or her home and the possibility of intruders, may repeatedly lock and relock the door when leaving the house or going to bed. Someone who is excessively distressed about germs may compulsively wash their hands over and over again throughout the day. The compulsive behaviors are not pleasurable and provide only temporary relief from the obsessive thoughts.

Some of the more commonly experienced obsessions are frequent thoughts of violent activities and harm to loved ones (although the individual would never act out these thoughts), thoughts of activities that would be contrary to the person's religious beliefs, and persistent thoughts of sexual acts, particularly those that the person dislikes. In addition, sufferers of OCD are often preoccupied with symmetry and order. They will arrange items in such a way that the spacing between them is exactly the same, colors are grouped together, or their houses are immaculately clean with nothing out of place. It is not uncommon for these individuals to have great difficulty throwing out things and to hoard items that are completely unnecessary, or to write down information that they will most likely never look at again such as license plate numbers, names, phone numbers on a passing billboard, or other such information.

Although even healthy individuals do, at times, perform rituals, such as checking several times to see if the windows are closed before leaving the house, those with OCD will perform these activities to such extremes that their normal functioning is interfered with. Most adults realize that their behavior is illogical, but they can't help themselves.

Approximately 2.2 million Americans suffer with OCD. Unfortunately, these people may also suffer with eating disorders, other anxieties, or depression at the same time. OCD may develop at any age and does not discriminate between men and women. There is also a strong likelihood that it runs in families. Treatment may be solely medicinal (to be discussed in chapter 4), behavioral, or a combination of the two.

## PANIC DISORDER

With panic disorder, another common form of anxiety, sufferers experience sudden attacks of terror often associated with physical symptoms such as faintness or dizziness, weakness, a pounding heart, and sweatiness. Individuals may feel chilled or flushed and experience tingling or numbness in their hands as well as feeling nauseous, having chest pain, or feeling as if they are smothering. The attacks also bring about a feeling of being out of control or of impending doom.

Unfortunately, panic attacks may occur at any time without provocation, even during sleep. They peak in about ten minutes, but, at times, may last much longer. They affect women twice as often as men and usually begin in late adolescence or early adulthood. A person may have only one panic attack in their lives without actually developing panic disorder. It is likely that the predisposition to develop full-blown panic disorder is inherited.

As with other forms of anxiety, people who have panic disorder will use avoidance techniques in an effort to avert an attack. This may seriously affect their lives as it may cause them to move out of an area, not take certain jobs, or avoid going to specific locations. For example, an individual who experienced a panic attack during a ride on the subway might completely avoid any further travel on that mode. This could make it difficult or impossible to get to work or go places where they might otherwise experience some form of entertainment such as a play or concert. In some cases, a person's life may be so disrupted that he or she becomes housebound and will not venture out at all or must be accompanied by a spouse or other trusted person. This condition is known as agoraphobia, meaning "fear of open spaces" or "fear of the marketplace."

Panic disorder affects approximately six million Americans and is one of the most treatable forms of anxiety affecting mankind. Some individuals will respond very well to cognitive therapy while others require only medication to control the attacks. Of course, there are those sufferers who do well with a combination of both therapies.

One of the unfortunate problems associated with panic disorder is that it is often accompanied by other conditions such as drug abuse, depression, or alcoholism. When the therapist treats these individuals, the accompanying conditions must be treated separately from the panic disorder.

## SPECIFIC PHOBIAS

Another group of disorders included in the spectrum of anxiety conditions is that of specific phobias. Approximately 19.2 million American adults suffer from these and, once again, they are twice as common in women. They usually begin in childhood or adolescence and continue on into adulthood. Why specific phobias occur is not clear, however, there seems to be a familial pattern to their development.

| | ECA Prevalence (%) (Epidemiologic Catchment Area) | NCS Prevalence (%) (National Comorbidity Study) | Best Estimate (%) |
|---|---|---|---|
| **Any Anxiety Disorder** | 13.1 | 18.7 | 16.4 |
| Simple Phobia | 8.3 | 8.6 | 8.3 |
| Social Phobia | 2.0 | 7.4 | 2.0 |
| Agoraphobia | 4.9 | 3.7 | 4.9 |
| GAD | (1.5)* | 3.4 | 3.4 |
| Panic Disorder | 1.6 | 2.2 | 1.6 |
| OCD | 2.4 | (0.9)* | 2.4 |
| PTSD | (1.9)* | 3.6 | 3.6 |
| **Any Mood Disorder** | 7.1 | 11.1 | 7.1 |
| Major Depressive (MD) Episode | 6.5 | 10.1 | 6.5 |
| Unipolar MD | 5.3 | 8.9 | 5.3 |
| Dysthymia | 1.6 | 2.5 | 1.6 |
| Bipolar I | 1.1 | 1.3 | 1.1 |
| Bipolar II | 0.6 | 0.2 | 0.6 |
| Schizophrenia | 1.3 | — | 1.3 |
| Nonaffective Psychosis | — | 0.2 | 0.2 |
| Somatization | 0.2 | — | 0.2 |
| Antisocial Personality Disorder (ASP) | 2.1 | — | 2.1 |
| Anorexia Nervosa | 0.1 | — | 0.1 |
| Severe Cognitive Impairment | 1.2 | — | 1.2 |
| **Any Disorder** | 19.5 | 23.4 | 21.0 |

## Table 3.1 Prevalence Rates of Disorders in Those Aged 18–54[14]

Source: U.S. Public Health Service. "Mental Health: A Report of the Surgeon General. Epidemiology of Mental Illness," March 31, 2009 (http://www.surgeongeneral.gov/library/mentalhealth/chapter2/sec2_1.html#epidemiology).
*Numbers in parentheses indicate prevalence of the disorder without any comorbidity.

Most people have specific concerns that persist throughout their lives, but with this condition, these fears are magnified, irrational, and usually pertain to something that poses little or no threat. There are several common phobias including those relating to elevators, heights, flying, spiders, dogs, tight spaces, and several others.

An interesting aspect of these phobias is that a particular phobia may not be all-encompassing. For example, an individual may be able to go snowboarding at the top of a mountain, but be unable to go any higher than the first floor of an apartment building. Why this occurs is unknown.

Once again, avoidance is an effective way of not allowing the phobia to affect one's life. However, if the act of avoiding the phobia impacts the person's ability to perform his or her job or interferes with his or her personal life, professional help is most definitely needed. In most cases, psychotherapy is the treatment of choice for this disorder.

## BIPOLAR DISORDER

Bipolar disorder, once called manic depression, is a mood disorder characterized by the occurrence of one or more episodes of abnormally elevated energy levels, mood and cognition, and one or more depressive episodes. When the patient is experiencing the elevated moods, he or she is said to be manic (or, experiencing mania) and when they convert to feelings of sadness, lack of energy, and hopelessness, they are suffering with depression. At times, a patient may also experience a mix of both types of symptoms at the same time. This is referred to as a mixed episode. It is not uncommon for any of these episodes to be separated by "normal" periods where the patient is not dealing with either of the two extremes. However, there are some patients who do not enter into a "normal" phase, but rather go back and forth rapidly between depression and mania. This type of activity is known as rapid cycling.

If a patient suffers with extreme manic episodes, they may experience psychotic symptoms such as hallucinations and delusions. Psychosis is characterized by a loss of contact with reality associated with thought disorders and personality changes. In addition, the patients may exhibit unusual or bizarre behavior.

Bipolar disorder has been subdivided into bipolar I, bipolar II and cyclothymia. Bipolar I disorder is associated with at least one manic or mixed episode. There may also be episodes of hypomania (a manic state that does not reach the same stage of dysfunction as a full manic episode) where they display a great deal of energy, but remain fully functional, as well as major depression. Drug induced bipolar disorder is not included. Treatment is often with lithium carbonate, a chemical that has been in use for many years to treat this form of the disorder.

Bipolar II disorder is characterized by at least one major depressive episode and at least one hypomanic episode. In this category, the major depressive episodes are more frequent and more intense than the manic episodes. Because hypomanic individuals may be highly functioning, this type of bipolar disorder is often under-diagnosed as the behavior of the individual is often overlooked as merely being over-achieving. Treatment of this form of bipolar disorder is usually with mood stabilizers such as any of several different anticonvulsants in conjunction with SSRIs. Lithium carbonate is also effective as a treatment.

Cyclothymia is actually a milder form of bipolar II disorder characterized by alternating mild hypomanic and depressive (dysthymic) episodes. The depression tends to be more chronic and low-level and a single hypomanic episode, in conjunction with this chronic depression, is enough to obtain a diagnosis of cyclothymia. Most people with cyclothymia are fully functioning and are sometimes even hyper-productive. Treatment once again utilizes lithium carbonate as well as some anticonvulsants, quetiapine (Seroquel) and clonazepam (Klonopin).

Regardless of which type of anxiety one suffers with, therapy, medication, and support are crucial in the recovery and treatment process. Support from family and friends and an association with one or more support groups make managing the conditions much easier.

# 4

# How Antidepressants and Antianxiety Drugs Work

*Marlene noticed that she was beginning to have difficulty cleaning out her office and throwing away old papers that she knew she would never need again. The thought of discarding them was making her feel uncomfortable to the point where she started to experience episodes of sweating, elevated heart and breathing rates, and an overall feeling of anxiety. Soon after, she found herself focusing on unimportant bits of information and going over them in her head again and again, always wishing that she could find out more about them even though they had no real bearing on her life.*

*Eventually, Marlene began to write down useless facts like license plate numbers of passing cars, names of people she didn't know that came up in casual conversations, and even unimportant facts that her friends might bring up when sitting down together to have coffee. She also would pick up empty gum wrappers, cigarette butts, and other refuse as she walked along the street on her way to the store, a friend's house, or any other destination.*

Marlene was suffering from obsessive-compulsive disorder (OCD), an anxiety disorder characterized by involuntary obsessive thoughts and compulsive behaviors that bring a small degree of calm to the sufferer for short periods of time. The individual is aware that he or she is acting in an unusual manner, but finds it virtually impossible to control. This makes it more frustrating than if the person were oblivious to their condition. They attempt to control the behavior and hide it from others so as to avoid embarrassment. At times, this is very difficult to do, especially when they are under stress and the condition worsens.

Obsessions take the form of recurrent thoughts that cause extreme anxiety and stress and are not about real-life problems. The individual is aware of the fact that they are unrealistic and tries to neutralize them with the repetitive actions, often to no avail. The repetitive acts are not at all related to the obsessive thoughts, but are a means of distraction from them.

Several antianxiety drugs are being used today to treat patients with OCD. Sometimes a drug is successful and other times very little is accomplished. Doctors often have to try one medication after the other in hopes that the drugs may help to improve the patient's condition.

## STRUCTURE AND FUNCTION OF THE NERVOUS SYSTEM

The nervous system is divided into two anatomical components: the central nervous system, which consists of the brain and spinal cord, and the peripheral nervous system, which includes all other nerves in the body. In this book, the emphasis will be on the central nervous system as the drugs being studied have a direct affect on the brain.

The human brain (Figure 4.1) contains approximately 100 billion neurons (nerves) and about 150 trillion synapses (the contact points between nerves).[1] The cortex, the region of the brain that makes up most of its mass, is divided into two hemispheres, a left and a right. This is the area of the brain that is responsible for thinking, reasoning, interpretation of senses, artistic appreciation, and a host of other functions.

The two hemispheres are connected by the corpus callosum, a structure made of nerve fibers covered with a fatty substance called myelin that helps nerves conduct impulses faster. All of the brain's activity is carried out by the billions of neurons that it contains. Each neuron communicates with other neurons at a junction known as the synapse. Here, chemicals called **neurotransmitters** fill the synapse gap so that nerve impulses may cross the space from one nerve to another or from a nerve to a muscle. In this way, the

## Brain Structures

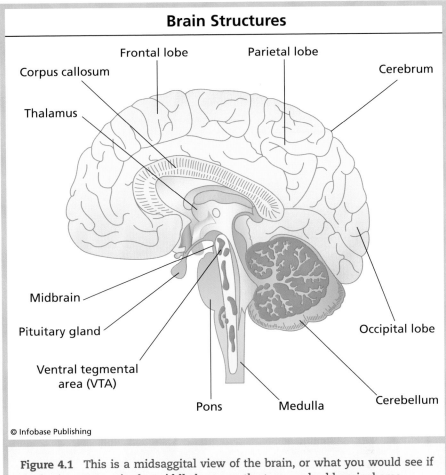

© Infobase Publishing

**Figure 4.1**  This is a midsaggital view of the brain, or what you would see if the brain were cut in the middle between the two cerebral hemispheres.

impulse can travel to its endpoint to cause a response in a muscle, gland, or organ or communication in the brain.

Because the brain has so many synapses and several of these neurotransmitters, many drugs may be used in different areas to bring about changes in the behavior of an individual. These drugs target the neurotransmitters themselves or they may mimic them so that a modification of the nerve impulse takes place. This activity is what hopefully brings about the desired change in behavior.

The mechanism whereby a nerve impulse is generated from one nerve to the next is very well designed A nerve impulse is carried along the axon of the presynaptic neuron (the nerve before the synapse) due to chemical changes

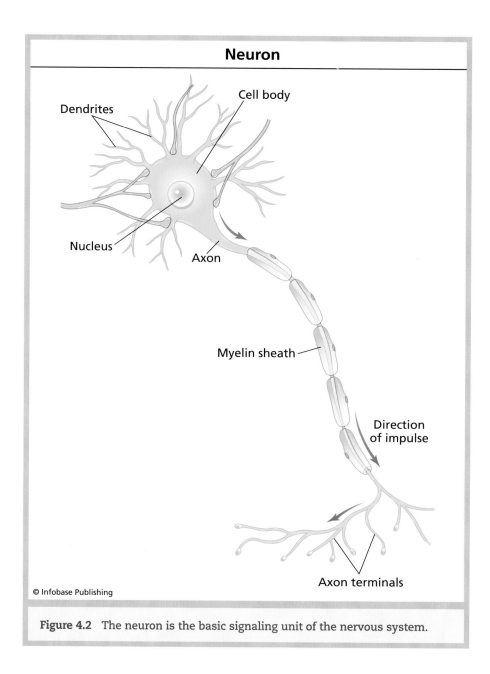

**Neuron**

Dendrites

Cell body

Nucleus

Axon

Myelin sheath

Direction of impulse

Axon terminals

© Infobase Publishing

**Figure 4.2**   The neuron is the basic signaling unit of the nervous system.

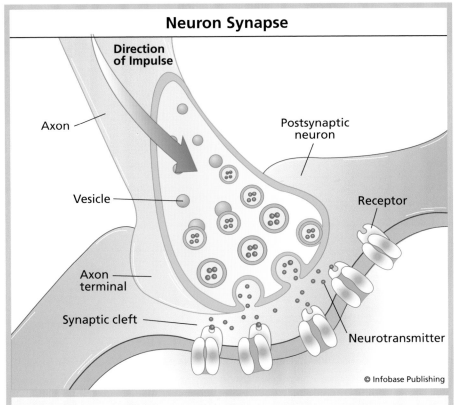

**Figure 4.3** Neurotransmitters are neurochemicals that diffuse across the synapse between the nerve ending of one neuron and the cell body of the next neuron and carry the neural signal to the receiving neuron.

particularly relating to the minerals sodium and potassium. At the end of the axon are axon terminals that contain vesicles filled with a specific neurotransmitter. Just beyond these terminals is a space, the synapse, which must be filled with a neurotransmitter so that the impulse can jump across and continue through the next nerve, the postsynaptic neuron (the nerve after the synapse).

The dendrites (small projections radiating from the nerve cell body) of the postsynaptic neuron contain receptors designed to capture the specific neurotransmitter, thus allowing the impulse to continue on its journey. Once the impulse stops, the neurotransmitter must be removed from the synapse. This

| Table 4.1 Brain Neruotransmitters and their Functions | |
|---|---|
| Acetylcholine | Generally excitatory |
| Aspartic Acid (Aspartate) | Excitatory |
| Dopamine | Inhibitory |
| Gamma Amino Butyric Acid (GABA) | Inhibitory |
| Glutamic Acid (Glutamate) | Excitatory |
| Glycine | Inhibitory |
| Norepinephrine | Excitatory |
| Peptides | Generally Inhibitory |
| Serotonin | Excitatory |

takes place in one of three ways, depending on the location of the synapse. For example, at the neuromuscular junction, the region where a nerve meets a muscle's motor endplate to stimulate contraction of the muscle, an enzyme known as acetylcholinesterase will enzymatically digest the neurotransmitter acetylcholine. In other synapses, simple diffusion (movement of the neurotransmitter molecules from a higher to a lower concentration) takes place.

In the brain, removal of the neurotransmitters is achieved by reuptake transporters that carry the neurotransmitter back into the axon terminal. This is where many of the medications used to treat depression and anxiety do their work. As these medicines interfere with the reuptake transporters, the specific neurotransmitter is allowed to remain in the synapse leading to continued transmission of impulses. This will modify a person's behavior since it is based on the numerous impulses that are transmitted from nerve to nerve through the synapses. The neurotransmitters are either excitatory, meaning that they stimulate an enhanced response, or inhibitory, meaning that they slow down a response. Some may play both roles depending on where they are doing their work.

This scenario of nerve impulse transmission takes place constantly throughout the body as long as an individual is alive, controlling the body's muscles, organs, and glands and functions of the brain and spinal cord. The nervous system works closely with the endocrine system, which is responsible for the secretion of many hormones. Together, they are often referred to as the neuroendocrine system.

# HOW ANTIDEPRESSANTS WORK

Since ancient times, physicians have attempted to heal the sick using spells, poultices, tinctures, potions, and any other compound they believed would be effective. Most of these were administered through the mouth as this is an easy way of introducing the medication to the body by allowing the digestive system to absorb it and the circulatory system to distribute it. With the invention of syringes, medications could be introduced into muscle or directly into the bloodstream via veins.

The medications used today to treat depression and anxiety are mostly in pill or capsule form and are taken at regular intervals by patients as directed by their physicians. Setting up a schedule helps people to remember when they should take their medication so that they can maintain fairly constant levels of medicine in their systems. This is extremely important when dealing with antidepressants and antianxiety drugs as a constant level of these ensures maximum effectiveness.

Today's medications for depression and anxiety are divided into several categories based on their mode of action. The drugs target either one specific neurotransmitter or several of them. In many of the cases, the drugs will interfere with the reuptake of the neurotransmitter at the synapse by blocking reuptake transporters.

Another way in which these medications act is by interfering with the enzyme monoamine oxidase. (See chapter 1 for a discussion of monoamine oxidase inhibitors, MAOIs.) This enzyme will catalyze the oxidation of neurotransmitters that fall into the category of monoamines such as serotonin and norepinephrine. Thus, MAOIs such as hydralazine (Apresoline), tranylcypromine (Parnate), and phenelzine (Nardil) will block the action of monoamine oxidase, allowing serotonin and norepinephrine to remain in the synapse propagating more impulses.

The tricyclic antidepressants (TCAs), first introduced in the 1950s, are another group of medications used to treat both depression and anxiety. They are categorized as tricyclic because their molecular structure includes three rings composed of carbon and nitrogen atoms. They function in a similar manner to some of the newer medications by inhibiting the reuptake of serotonin and norepinephrine. In recent years TCAs have been replaced by the more modern selective serotonin, norepinephrine dopamine, and serotonin/norepinephrine reuptake inhibitors, as these have fewer side effects.

The **selective serotonin reuptake inhibitors (SSRIs)** act exactly as their name implies. They selectively block the reuptake of only serotonin at the synapses in the brain where serotonin is the neurotransmitter used to conduct the impulse.

Similar to these are the **serotonin-norepinephrine reuptake inhibitors (SNRIs)** that act to block the reuptake of both serotonin and norepinephrine in the brain synapses.

Along the same lines, there are dopamine reuptake inhibitors (DRIs) that act only on dopamine reuptake in the synapse and norepinephrine dopamine reuptake inhibitors (NDRIs) that block the reuptake of both neurotransmitters.

## HOW ANTIANXIETY DRUGS WORK

As might be expected, different categories of antianxiety drugs have different modes of action. Because the brain is such a complex structure, there are several approaches to reducing or eliminating anxiety.

Benzodiazepines, such as Valium and Klonopin, reduce anxiety by depressing the central nervous system. They achieve this by binding to receptors for the neurotransmitter gamma amino butyric acid (GABA) and giving them a stronger affinity for it. Because GABA is an inhibitory neurotransmitter, its action is enhanced and the nervous system is "slowed down," thus reducing the anxiety.

Barbiturates, including phenobarbital, pentobarbital, and secobarbital among others, act to reduce anxiety in two different ways at the same time. Just like benzodiazepines, they too bind to GABA receptors causing them to attach more strongly to the neurotransmitter. In addition, barbiturates block receptors for the neurotransmitter glutamate, which is excitatory. Thus, they are enhancing central nervous system inhibition and blocking stimulation as well. This makes them very potent as sedatives and contributes to their history of being highly addictive.

Another group of antianxiety drugs works by enhancing serotonin's inhibitory effects. The drug BuSpar most likely works directly on a serotonin

| Table 4.2 Side Effects of Some Common Antidepressants and Antianxiety Medications* | |
| --- | --- |
| SSRIs: Prozac, Zoloft, Paxil, Celexa, Luvox, and others | Headaches, nausea, diarrhea, loss of libido, worry, insomnia, anxiety, nervousness, fatigue, drowsiness, abnormal dreams, abnormal thoughts |
| SNRIs: Pristiq, Cymbalta, Effexor, and others | Generally similar to side effects seen with SSRIs; change in appetite, drowsiness, dizziness, fatigue, headache, reduced libido, urinary retention, mildly elevated blood pressure |
| DRIs and NDRIs: Ritalin, Meridia (weak DRI), Wellbutrin (NDRI) | Dizziness, abdominal pain, cardiac arrhythmias (irregular heartbeats), nausea, rapid heartbeat, headaches, dry mouth, sweating, possible seizures with high doses |
| Tricyclic Antidepressants (TCAs): Elavil, Anafranil, Tofranil, and others | Blurred vision, weight changes, dry mouth, sexual problems, dizziness, drowsiness, rashes |
| Monoamine Oxidase Inhibitors (MAOIs): Apresoline, Parnate, Nardil, Marplan, and others | Dry mouth, dizziness, headache, drowsiness, insomnia, sexual problems, liver inflammation, heart attack, seizures, or stroke. MAOI users avoid smoked, pickled, or fermented foods and other sources of tyramine, a fermentation product of the amino acid tyrosine. A buildup of tyramine will cause severe hypertension. |
| Antianxiety Medications- Lexapro, BuSpar, Klonopin, Luvox, Valium, Serax, Tranxene, Miltown, and others | Dry mouth, drowsiness, dizziness, fatigue, weakness, nausea, blurred vision, decreased coordination, constipation |

*Not every drug causes the same side effects. Different drugs are associated with a different assortment of the side effects listed here. In addition, many of these drugs will cause the same side effects.

receptor known as 5-HT1A, making serotonin's inhibitory effects on the central nervous system much stronger, thus reducing anxiety while it promotes normal sleeping and eating patterns. Serotonin activity is also modified by those SSRIs that work on anxiety as they block the reuptake of serotonin from the synapses, causing it to remain there for an extended period of time. This condition enhances its inhibitory effects and reduces anxiety.

Pregabalin, a drug generally used as an anticonvulsant, has also been used to treat generalized anxiety disorder. It works by decreasing the release of the neurotransmitters norepinephrine and glutamate, both of which are excitatory. At the same time it increases GABA levels bringing about inhibition. Its potential for abuse is quite low, making it safer than benzodiazepines and barbiturates.

## THE PLACEBO EFFECT

A placebo is a substance that has no true pharmaceutical effect, but which will bring about the desired response in a patient because he or she expects it to work. Of course, the patient is not told in advance that the "drug" is really an inert substance. The word comes from the Latin word *placebo* that is translated to "I shall please." Over the years, placebos have been used to treat inflammation, pain, depression, anxiety, Parkinson's disease and even cancer.[2] The effect may occur because the patient truly believes that the "medicine" he or she is being given will work to help alleviate the problem, or, some degree of success may be achieved based on a subconscious association between recovery and the act of being treated.

The effect has been shown to arise from active processes in the brain. It may actually enhance immune responses and hormonal release. In the eighteenth century, many physicians would use inert substances to treat patients when they had no effective drugs that would combat a disease or condition. They felt that the patient must receive something since he or she went out of their way to visit the doctor and surely expected to be cured.

An interesting experiment was performed at the University of Duisberg-Essen in Germany and the Swiss Federal Institute of Technology Zurich to prove the placebo effect. Rats were given the immunosuppressive drug cyclosporine A. This medication is used to suppress the immune system following a transplant so that the rejection rate is slowed down. At the same time that the cyclosporine was administered, the rats were also given water sweetened with saccharin. Apparently, the rats associated the cyclosporine with the sweet taste of the water because, later on, when the rats were given only saccharin-sweetened water, their immune systems became suppressed. Some subconscious cue told the brain to signal the immune system to partially shut down. This shows that an individual might get relief from a placebo without consciously believing that it will be effective in treating his or her condition.

A similar experiment was later performed at the University of Duisberg-Essen on humans. 18 healthy men were given capsules of cyclosporine A over three days along with a greenish strawberry milkshake that smelled of lavender. Because of the cyclosporine A, their immune systems showed signs of reduced activity. Five days later, the subjects took dummy capsules along with the same drink. Once again, their immune systems showed signs of becoming depressed, but not as much as they had when the real cyclosporine A was administered. As a control, 16 men received only dummy pills throughout the experiment and showed no signs of a suppressed immune system.

Studies of the placebo effect as it relates to depression have shown that 50–65% of patients respond to antidepressant medications while 25–30% respond to a placebo.[3] Furthermore, it has been shown that a number of patients who respond to treatment in the initial phase of therapy experience a relapse or recurrence even as treatment is continuing. It has been suggested that this is related to the placebo effect as the patients respond in the beginning because they expect the drugs to alleviate the symptoms of the depression even though, in reality, they are not really helping the condition.

The placebo effect has also been shown to work when anxiety is being treated. In a Swedish study[4], volunteers were shown a series of unpleasant pictures designed to cause feelings of anxiety. The volunteers were asked to

| Table 4.3 Placebo Medicine | | |
|---|---|---|
| Disease | Average Percentage of Patients in Whom Placebo Therapy Worked | Number of Studies; Total Number of Participants |
| Cancer | 2–7 (tumors reduced in size) | 10; 464 |
| Crohn's Disease | 19 | 32; 1,047 |
| Chronic Fatigue Syndrome | 19.6 | 29; 1,016 |
| Duodenal Ulcer | Healing in 36.2–44.2 | 79; 3,325 |
| Irritable Bowel Syndrome | 40 | 45; 3,193 |
| Multiple Sclerosis | 11–50 (fewer episodes after two to three years) | 6; 264 |

Source: Maj-Britt Niemi. "Placebo Effect: A cure in the Mind." Scientific American Mind," pp. 42–49, February, 2009. Available online. URL: http://www.scientificamerican.com/article.cfm?id=placebo-effect-a-cure-in-the-mind. Accessed on July 7, 2010.

rate their anxiety on a scale of 0–100. They were then given benzodiazepine, a legitimate antianxiety drug, and told it would reduce their anxiety. The volunteers reported a decrease in anxiety levels from an average of 51 down to an average of 29. They were then given an antidote to the benzodiazepine and their anxiety levels reached an average of 61.

The following day, the same volunteers were tested in the same way and told that they were being given the same drugs as the day before. However, both drugs were merely placebos. The results were basically the same. The anxiety level dropped from 51 to 36 after they received the placebo antianxiety drug and returned to 51 after receiving the fake antidote.

## A SERIOUS PROBLEM

Since 2003, doctors, pharmaceutical companies and the Food and Drug Administration have been aware that several antidepressants have the potential to cause an increased risk of suicidal thoughts and actions in children who use these drugs. Included in the list are Celexa (citalopram), Effexor (venlafaxine), Lexapro (escitalopram), Luvox (fluvoxamine), Paxil (paroxetine), Prozac (fluoxetine), Remeron (mirtazapine), Serzone (nefazodone), Wellbutrin, Zyban (bupropion), and Zoloft (sertraline). There were no suicides during the clinical trials and it was unclear to the FDA as to whether or not there were actual suicide attempts or simply self-injurious behavior that was not related to suicide.[5]

As a result of these findings, a "black box" warning has been placed on these medications (since September 14, 2004) to inform the prescribing physicians that the medications should not be used in children under 18 years of age. This type of warning is the most serious type and, although it does not make it illegal to write a prescription for a child, it clearly advises against it. The warning specifically cites the fact that the drugs are associated with suicidal behavior in 4% of those children who used them compared to 2% of children given a placebo.[6]

Apparently, the suicide rate among adults taking antidepressants may also be elevated. In a study performed at the Institute for Forensic Medicine in Munich, Germany, 10% of the suicides investigated between 2001–2005 were associated with individuals who were taking one of several different categories of antidepressants.[7] The youngest victim taking SSRIs was 28 years old.

# 5
# The Treatment Process

*Sandra suffered from depression for many years. As a child, she often exhibited the signs and symptoms of depression. This was not surprising as her father and grandfather also had suffered with depression from the time they were young adults. Apparently, there was a genetic link that ran in the family, making it very difficult for Sandra to avoid becoming depressed.*

*Over the years, Sandra was treated by several psychiatrists who used a combination of psychotherapy (once called the "talking cure" by Sigmund Freud) and different antidepressant drugs. However, no matter which drugs Sandra was taking and how many hours she spent with her therapists, she still suffered repeated serious bouts of depression.*

*Now in her forties, Sandra was despondent and felt resigned to the fact that she might never get better and live a normal life. She often contemplated suicide and mentioned to her friends that she would be better off dead than feeling as miserable as she did.*

*Finally, her psychiatrist suggested that she begin a treatment regimen with scopolamine, a drug that had been used for years to treat nausea and motion sickness, but was now being used as an antidepressant that recently showed an ability to work quickly and yielded excellent results.[1] At first Sandra was resistant as she was concerned about possible side effects. Nevertheless, she was desperate and agreed to begin taking the medication.*

*After only a few days, Sandra began to experience fewer and less severe episodes of depression. Understandably, her outlook on life improved and she no longer thought about suicide. She became more outgoing and participated in more activities with family and friends. Hers was truly a success story brought about by beginning to take a previously untried medication.*

If an individual is suffering from depression, anxiety, or both, he or she should immediately consult their family physician. If the physician feels that the patient is in need of a specialist, a referral will be made to a psychiatrist or psychologist. The psychiatrist is able to prescribe the proper medication to go along with the form of behavioral therapy employed with the individual patient. A psychologist is not licensed to prescribe medications, but will rely on different forms of behavioral modification in an effort to help the patient. If these are deemed insufficient, a referral to a psychiatrist is usually made so that medication may be added to the treatment regimen.

## PSYCHOTHERAPY

Psychotherapy is a form of personal counseling provided by a psychiatrist, psychologist, clinical social worker, or other health care professional where the patient and therapist develop an interpersonal relationship in an effort to help the patient come to terms with problems that are having a major impact on his or her life. Treatment may be carried out with or without the use of medications. The ultimate goal is to increase the patient's sense of well-being.

Many different techniques are used by therapists to achieve the goals established at the beginning of the therapy sessions. Some of these include cognitive behavioral therapy (CBT), psychoanalysis, group psychotherapy, behavior therapy, and hypnotherapy.

## COGNITIVE BEHAVIORAL THERAPY (CBT)

This approach to treating anxiety and depression began as a combining of behavioral therapy and cognitive therapy. Behavioral therapy was developed in the early 20th century and cognitive therapy began in the 1960s.

In the 1950s, Dr. Albert Ellis developed a technique that he called rational therapy, which was an early form of CBT. This treatment regimen was an active-directive form of therapy designed to resolve emotional and behavioral problems, thus allowing individuals to lead more normal and satisfying lives.

In the 1960s, Dr. Aaron T. Beck, inspired by Ellis' work, developed cognitive therapy. This technique is designed to first identify dysfunctional thinking in a patient and then to change it along with dysfunctional behavior and emotions. The therapist challenges the patient by pointing out what is wrong with his or her thinking, thus allowing the patient's feelings to be more easily changed.

Cognitive behavioral therapy has been shown to be effective in treating several different psychological problems including anxiety, substance abuse, and eating disorders.[2]

# PSYCHOANALYSIS

This form of treatment was developed in the 1800s by Sigmund Freud. He felt that the mind consisted of three parts: the self-gratifying id, the rational ego, and the moral superego. The approach is to look into a person's unconscious mind to find out why he or she is having difficulties. He felt that the unconscious mind is influenced by childhood experiences, so he often attempted to find out about events in a patient's past that would influence their behavior. Although behavior is frequently a target in therapy, many therapeutic techniques focus on feelings and thoughts.

# GROUP PSYCHOTHERAPY

This form of psychotherapy began in the early 20th century with the term first used around 1920 when Jacob L. Moreno developed the technique of psychodrama in which a group of patients would act as both cast and audience in a "play" reenacting problems under the direction of the therapist.[3]

Group psychotherapy continued to become more popular in Europe throughout the 20th century and eventually was brought to the United States where it is still used today in many locations. Groups don't necessarily employ the use of psychodrama, but a therapist acts as the moderator of the group and all of the patients interact. This form of therapy has proven to be very successful in some cases.

# BEHAVIOR THERAPY

The goal of behavior therapy is to modify a patient's behavior in an effort to achieve a goal. Both operant and respondent conditioning are employed

## THE TALKING CURE

Sigmund Freud (1856–1939) tried many different techniques to treat different patients with various psychological disorders. He tried to use hypnosis to treat his patients and found that the results were less than satisfactory. He turned to a technique where the patient talked through his or her problems. This technique, originally called the "talking cure" by a patient Anna O. who was treated by Freud's colleague Josef Breuer, was designed to bring out repressed and rejected thoughts and fears so that a cure could be achieved. This was the basis for modern psychotherapy.

**Figure 5.1.  Sigmund Freud.**  *(National Library of Medicine)*

in this technique. Sometimes this approach is integrated with cognitive therapy—creating cognitive behavioral therapy. Behavioral therapies are focused on a patient's environment and way of life and what particular consequence or effect a specific behavior will have. The ultimate goal is to modify the behavior so that a negative consequence does not result.

## HYPNOTHERAPY

Practitioners using this form of psychotherapy will hypnotize the patient to bring about a change in a particular behavior or attitude. In addition, the technique has been used successfully to eliminate dysfunctional habits and personality traits such as smoking, overeating, loss of self-confidence, and even anxiety.

## EMERGENCY CARE OF THE DEPRESSED PATIENT

When an individual experiences a serious depressive episode, time is of the essence in providing emergency treatment to help the patient avoid attempting suicide and to improve the patient's mood to the point where he or she is able to function reasonably normally.

Major depressive episodes are associated with higher suicide rates in young adults and the elderly, although both may occur in any age group including children.[4] In addition, when a patient presents with drug or alcohol abuse or overdose, or a self-inflicted injury, the individual must be screened for major depression and suicidality.

In cases where it appears that there is a strong possibility the patient is suicidal, the individual must be hospitalized with his or her own consent, or he or she may be admitted via emergency commitment. If there is assurance that the patient's safety may be guaranteed, he or she will be treated as an outpatient and may come and go to the hospital or a psychiatrist's office where psychotherapy and drug treatment will be used. If a child attempts suicide, he or she is usually placed in a protected environment until such time that both medical treatment and social services are in place.

In some cases, electroconvulsive therapy (also called ECT or electroshock therapy) is used to treat the patient immediately after release from the emergency room. This is usually used when the patient has not responded to medications administered in the emergency room or has had an adverse reaction to these

## TIMELINE OF THE DEVELOPMENT OF ELECTROCONVULSIVE THERAPY

**1938:** Development of electroconvulsive therapy (ECT)
**1940s–1960s:** Increased use of ECT especially for treating depression
**1960s–1970s:** Decrease in use of ECT due to improved medications and stigma associated with ECT treatment
**1970s–Present:** Increased use of ECT for depression and other psychiatric disorders due to improvements in overall technique

medications or where the depression is so severe that it must be reversed immediately. Usually, a psychiatrist is called in to set up a treatment plan.

Electroconvulsive therapy was first introduced in the 1930s and was used quite extensively in the 1940s and 1950s. It is estimated that today approximately one million people worldwide undergo this form of treatment for depression each year.[5] ECT is used as a "last resort" for patients whose depression does not respond to conventional pharmaceutical and psychotherapeutic treatments. It is considered controversial as it induces seizures in an anaesthetized patient in an effort to bring about a degree of regulation of brain chemistry. In addition, the actual mechanism of action is not truly understood. Nevertheless, one study showed that this form of treatment was the most effective in bringing about significant improvements in patients' long- and short-term quality of life.[6]

## EMERGENCY TREATMENT OF ANXIETY

Anxiety attacks are often accompanied by several physical signs and symptoms affecting different systems of the body; for example, rapid heartbeat (tachycardia), rapid breathing (tachypnea), elevated blood pressure, and possibly several others. Along with the anxiety, these conditions must be addressed as well.

It is not unusual for the emergency room physicians to initially treat a patient suffering an anxiety attack with a benzodiazepine (Valium, Librium,

Klonopin, Xanax, etc.).[7] This type of medication is used to calm the person and help alleviate some of the associated signs and symptoms mentioned above. Benzodiazepines are short-acting and highly therapeutic. Barbiturates [phenobarbital, pentobarbital (Nembutal), secobarbital (Seconal and others)] are not generally used because they are highly addictive, slow to act, and have many side effects. Of course, if the symptoms are severe, an immediate psychiatric consult is called for in addition to medications.

Because abnormal vital signs are commonly associated with anxiety attacks, emergency treatment must include careful monitoring of these signs. Blood pressure should be measured several times, especially after medication has been administered, to ensure that any elevation was directly associated with the attack. If the pressure does not return to normal as the patient calms down, true hypertension must be considered and treated accordingly. Initial tachycardia often subsides as the patient is reassured, but if it does not, other causes must be explored and treated.

To help calm the patient, a quiet room should be provided so an accurate evaluation may be made of the patient's condition. However, most hospitals don't have such areas available. In fact, the environment of an emergency room often helps to increase the patient's anxiety level. In addition, the extensive time often spent in the waiting room acts to increase anxiety.

In cases of chronic anxiety, the level of intensity is usually lower. These patients may be treated with different antianxiety drugs than those used for acute cases. The best pharmacotherapy will be determined by a psychiatrist who is seeing the patient on a regular basis outside of the hospital setting.

## OUTPATIENT TREATMENT

Once an emergency patient is stabilized or if a patient is merely suffering from depression or anxiety and has not had to visit an emergency room as his or her level of these conditions isn't life-threatening, outpatient treatment becomes crucial. A variety of medications as well as psychotherapy may be prescribed by a psychiatrist in the office to determine why the patient is suffering and what may be done about it.

Before the invention of the medications that are used to treat psychiatric conditions, psychotherapy was employed by psychiatrists and psychologists to treat their patients. Psychotherapy is basically the development of an interpersonal relationship between the therapist and the patient that will help the individual who has difficulties dealing with life. Sigmund Freud, perhaps the father of modern psychotherapy, referred to this relationship as the "talking cure." A number of different techniques are employed including communication, dialogue, behavioral modification, and relationship building. Whatever technique is employed, the aim is to improve the mental health of the patient or help the individual with group relationships.

Most psychiatrists and psychotherapists will use some form of oral communication to work with the patient. However, this is not the only means of attempting to help with the individual's problems. Other techniques include artwork, music, narrative stories, and a variety of approaches designed to help the patient understand the causes of the anxiety or depression and find a way to deal with these causes.

## THE HOLISTIC APPROACH

In addition to the techniques for treating anxiety and depression already mentioned, many patients seek out more natural approaches to treatment. These techniques are based on the belief that the mind and the body are not separate entities, but rather that the systems of the body and the mind constantly communicate and interact with each other in a sort of holistic network that includes hormones, metabolism, and biochemistry. What this means is that a problem in one area of the body will have an effect on other areas as well.

One natural "medicine" that has been used for many years is the herb St. John's Wort (hypericum). It works by increasing the activity of norepinephrine and serotonin (because it acts as a weak MAOI), which is why doctors use SNRIs to treat patients with depression.

Another biochemical approach to treating depression is through the use of inositol and omega-3 fatty acids. Inositol works similarly to St. John's Wort by increasing the levels of serotonin. Studies have shown that inositol helped to relieve symptoms of depression.[8] Omega-3 fatty acid supplementation was discovered to improve symptoms of depression as well as being able to treat schizophrenia, bipolar disorder, eating disorders, and attention deficit/hyperactivity disorder.[9]

The amino acid tryptophan has also been shown to help alleviate symptoms of depression because it is used by the body in producing serotonin.[10]

Once again, as long as there are sufficient amounts of serotonin in the synapses of the brain, the symptoms of depression may be alleviated.

Another herb, Gingko Biloba, is known to help improve blood circulation. By this action, it has been shown to be useful in treating cases of depression

**Figure 5.2**  St. John's wort, a plant that has been used as an herbal anti-depressant. *(U.S. Department of Agriculture)*

that may be caused by cerebral insufficiency due to reduced blood flow to the brain.[11]

Kanna (*Sceletium tortuosum*) has been used to treat depression as well.[12] This plant grows in South Africa and contains mesembrine, a chemical that acts as a phosphodiesterase (PDE4) inhibitor. This enzyme normally breaks down intracellular chemicals including some found in the nervous system. By blocking PDE4, these chemicals are made more available to the nerves and symptoms of depression may be alleviated.

The nutritional supplement SAM-e (S-adenosylmethionine) has also been used to treat depression. This product is a synthetic form of a compound found in the body made from the amino acid methionine and adenosine triphosphate (ATP), the body's natural energy chemical. It is suggested that this compound increases the availability of serotonin and dopamine.[13]

In addition to biochemical approaches to treating depression, a change in lifestyle has also been shown to be effective in helping to alleviate symptoms. Gardening, meditating, burning frankincense (resin from the Boswellia plant), body movement (walking, running, exercising), and laughing have all been shown to help relieve depression in many individuals.[14]

Anxiety may also be treated by holistic methods. Several herbs and supplements have been used as a treatment, including GABA, passion flower, valerian, Ashwagandha, and L-Threonine.[15] Gamma amino butyric acid (GABA) is an inhibitory neurotransmitter. Some research has shown that adding this as a supplement to the diet can help to alleviate mild anxiety.

Passion flower (*Passiflora incarnata L*) extract has been used for years to "calm jittery nerves" in over-the-counter products. Animal studies have shown that the extract will work to calm agitated animals.

The use of valerian (*Valeriana officinalis*) to treat anxiety dates back to the ancient Chinese and Greeks. Valerian interacts with GABA to bring about a mild sedative action. Patients who don't exercise, who can't calm down mentally, and who exhibit stress along with despondency and mental depression have responded best to valerian.

Ashwagandha (*Withania somnifera*) has been used extensively in Indian Ayurvedic medicine. Research has revealed that this plant helps to bring about both physical and mental well-being. In fact, it was able to bring about almost the same relief as some benzodiazepines and tricyclic antidepressants.

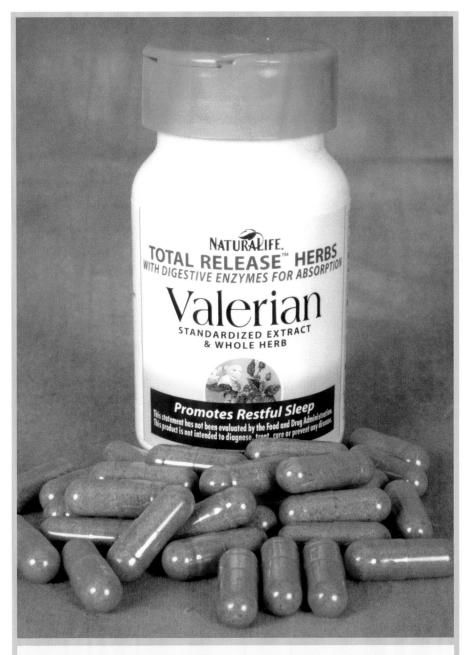

**Figure 5.3**  Valerian is a plant that has been used an herbal antianxiety drug.
(© *Custom Medical Stock Photo*)

## DEPRESSION SUPPORT GROUPS: A NECESSARY PART OF SUCCESSFUL TREATMENT

Due to the prevalence of depression in our society, numerous support groups have been formed. These are crucial in helping those with depression find strength in overcoming their condition. Some of these groups include

- Depression Forums
- Find the Light
- Depression-and-Anxiety-Recovery.com
- Depression Understood
- HelpingTeens.org
- New Directions Support Group

There are, of course, many other groups available both online and accessible through local mental health facilities and health departments.

The amino acid L-Threonine is found in green tea. It, too, has been shown to help alleviate some of the symptoms of anxiety. It induces a state of relaxation by causing the production of alpha brain waves and it is involved in the production of GABA. Because GABA helps to influence the levels of serotonin and dopamine, the relaxing effect is achieved.

## EFFECTIVENESS OF TREATMENT

From a statistical standpoint, antidepressants are effective in controlling depression in approximately one third of cases, have partial success in another third, and have no effect at all in the last third.[16] When drugs alone are used, relapses are common. Treatments such as cognitive behavioral therapy have been shown to have a 70% success rate in preventing relapses. This success rate is related to cases of depression that are not caused strictly by a chemical imbalance, but are the result of an individual's response to a stressful situation.

CBT helps them to learn how to respond in a different fashion so that depression doesn't occur.

In cases of anxiety, the results are similar to those associated with depression. Once again, in addition to pharmaceutical therapy, some form of behavioral therapy is needed to become symptom free and stay that way. In most cases, drugs alone are not sufficient to cure the patient.

With diligent attention from the health care provider, patient compliance in relation to taking medications, and going to scheduled therapy sessions, many individuals will be successful in overcoming anxiety and depression.

# 6

# Antidepressants and Antianxiety Drugs and Society

*Steve and Sally had been married for 25 years. Their relationship was a good one and they enjoyed going out as a family with their two children to many different restaurants, vacations, and amusement areas. One cool, sunny day in early October, Sally began to feel "strange." She found that she was beginning to lose interest in the family activities she once enjoyed. Over time she lost her appetite, found it difficult to go to work in the morning, and was unable to find any activities that entertained her or made her feel fulfilled.*

*Because of this change in Sally's personality, Steve and the children began to feel a sense of loss as they didn't go out as a family like they used to since they felt that it would be wrong to leave Sally home while they were out enjoying themselves. A general sense of longing for the "good old days" overcame the entire family as they realized that Sally was suffering from clinical depression and, unless therapy was begun, those days would never come again.*

## ANXIETY AND DEPRESSION: AFFECTING THOSE AROUND THE SUFFERER

Unfortunately, anxiety and depression have far-reaching effects. Not only does the sufferer have to deal with these conditions, but those who are associated with him or her are also affected. The lives of the caregivers, such as spouses, parents, siblings, and children are all impacted when someone near them suffers.

It is often difficult for those around the sufferer to ignore what is going on. Because individuals with these conditions are not able to function normally, they impose restrictions on close relatives and friends. For example, a person with agoraphobia often cannot go out of the house. A spouse would then be unable to go to a movie, restaurant, or even visit friends unless he or she goes alone. This would undoubtedly cause problems as the sufferer would feel abandoned and jealous that he or she could not join in on the activity.

A severely depressed individual, because of his or her inability to become motivated to do work, might be unable to go to their job and force a spouse to take on extra employment to cover everyday expenses. In addition, the spouse might also have to do the shopping and house cleaning as the sufferer might also be unable to motivate themselves to do these tasks.

Of course, depending on the specific situation, there are a number of effects that depression and anxiety may have on those who are close to individuals with these conditions. Because each case is somewhat unique, it would be impossible to describe all of the possible situations that might arise. Regardless, no one will deny that those with depression and anxiety will have a profound affect on anyone close to them in one way or another.

The prevalence of depression and anxiety in the United States alone is alarming. More than one in twenty Americans 12 years of age and older suffer with depression.[1] Worldwide, the World Health Organization found that major depression was the leading cause of disability.[2]

Depression and anxiety may strike anyone, anywhere, but studies have shown that certain ethnic, socioeconomic, and age-related groups are more prone to developing these ailments.

One study showed that two thirds of Canadians have had some experience with depression or anxiety while 36% actually suffered from it themselves.[3] In addition, two thirds of Canadians know someone who has suffered from anxiety or depression. In this same study, participants were asked whether they thought that depression and anxiety had an impact on society as a whole: 79% responded that the impact was strong. When looking specifically at the effects of depression and anxiety on personal relationships, 86% felt there was a strong impact on relationships with family and friends. In relation to employment, 78% believed the two conditions had a strong impact on a person's success at their job. And, when it came to how others would view an individual with depression or anxiety, only one third of the participants believed people would think less of them if they suffered from depression or anxiety.

The Canadian study also looked at how often people with anxiety and depression actually sought treatment. Half of the respondents who felt they had suffered from depression or anxiety had never sought medical help, with men being less likely than women to see a doctor (39% versus 56%).

A study carried out by the National Institute of Mental Health (NIMH) in the United States looked at several different statistics associated with depression. The study revealed that major depressive disorder is the leading cause of disability among Americans between the ages of 15 and 44.[4] This translates to approximately 17.1 million American adults ages 18 and older annually. The median age of onset was found to be 32.5 years old; it was twice as common in women as in men.

The study also showed that depression is also a serious problem in the elderly. Of the approximately 35 million Americans aged 65 and older, about 2 million are suffering from major depressive disorder. Another five million experience less serious depression. If gone untreated, both the individual and their family will suffer needlessly. Also, untreated depression may lead to suicide.

One of the problems experienced particularly by the elderly with depression is that often depression may coexist with physical ailments such as stroke, heart attack, cancer, diabetes, and Parkinson's disease. The patient, doctor, and family might mistake this depression as being entirely related to the physical condition when, in fact, it is a separate entity. If this is the case, the depression may go untreated. This is unfortunate as treatment might help alleviate the symptoms, thus making the patient's life, and that of those around him or her, somewhat better.

The same situation exists in reference to economic status. Many elderly Americans, as well as those in other countries, are on a fixed income. This severely limits their lifestyles and can bring about depression. Once again, if they are in this situation, but are also suffering from a true case of depression, it might go untreated.

Health care costs are much higher among older adults suffering with depression in addition to other medical conditions. One study showed that Medicare participants suffering with congestive heart failure or diabetes in addition to depression have significantly higher health care costs than their counterparts who were not suffering with depression. Participants in an NIMH study who suffered with depression had average annual health care costs of $22,960 whereas those without depression incurred costs of $11,956. Those diagnosed with possible depression spent $14,365.[5]

Suicide, as a result of depression, is a major concern among practitioners, patients, families, and friends. More men than women die from suicide, but women attempt suicide twice as often. In addition, depression affects twice as many women as men.[6]

Childhood depression has come to light in the past two decades. The condition may affect feelings, behavior, and the physical state of the individual. In children, the symptoms appear to be more intense and last longer than in adults. Children suffering from depression have a difficult time dealing with daily responsibilities and activities and are prone to struggles relating to their schoolwork, behavior at home, interactions with others, and self-esteem.

Depression in teenagers is also a serious problem. Studies have shown that at any time, 10–15% of children and adolescents exhibit various symptoms of depression. The occurrence rate among teenagers is very close to that in adults and may be as high as one in eight. Suicide in teenagers is a serious problem in that thousands of teens commit suicide each year in the United States.[7] It is the third leading cause of death among 15–24-year-olds and the sixth leading cause of death among 5–14-year-olds.

Anxiety disorders are also a very serious societal problem. They are the most common mental illness in the United States, affecting approximately 40 million adults aged 18 and older.[8] They cost more than $42 billion per year, which includes the cost of treatment for bodily complaints that mimic actual physical illnesses. This puts a very heavy burden on the health care system and on the patient's family and friends. In addition, it affects the individual's ability to perform his or her daily work and social activities and responsibilities.

## MEDICINE AND TREATMENT ARE EXPENSIVE

As noted above, the cost of treating individuals with depression and/or anxiety can be prohibitive. Each patient requires one or more medications and should also be receiving psychotherapy so that the medications alone aren't expected to bring about significant improvement.

Retail prices for commonly prescribed antidepressants range from about $20 per month to as high as $400 per month.[9] Of course, buying generic versions of the brand name drugs will always be cheaper because the manufacturers of brand name drugs must include the cost of research and development in the sale price of their medications. Once the patent has expired, other pharmaceutical manufacturers may produce generic forms of the original medications. These forms must conform to federal guidelines and be virtually the same as the original drugs. There has been much controversy surrounding the efficacy of generic drugs. Many wonder whether they are as good as the originals in remedying the conditions they are meant to treat.

According to Blue Cross Blue Shield of Michigan, a 1% increase in the sales of generic drugs would save subscribers $30 million.[10] This is helpful both to the individual subscribers in that it keeps their premiums down and to the insurance companies as it keeps their expenditures at a lower level. Table 6.1 shows the great disparity between the cost of name-brand drugs and their generic counterparts.

When it comes to psychotherapy, there is also a very large expenditure. The costs of an office visit may be prohibitive to the majority of people who don't have health insurance. Fees will vary based on the location of the office. For example, fees in large cities like New York, Los Angeles, San Francisco and Chicago are higher than those in small towns in Iowa or South Dakota. In the San Francisco Bay area, for example, psychiatrists typically charge anywhere from $125 per hour to $285 per hour. Psychologists' fees range from $90 to $150 per hour and Marriage, Family, and Child counselor fees are approximately $100 per hour.[11]

Before the 1990s, psychiatrists and psychotherapists were able to charge higher fees to patients with insurance coverage than they can today. This is because managed care programs were instituted by the insurance carriers. The programs were designed to reduce costs to the companies. A practitioner

| Table 6.1 Comparison of Costs between Brand Name Drugs and Generic Drugs | | | | | |
|---|---|---|---|---|---|
| Brand Name/ Strength* | Commonly Prescribed Quantity (30 day supply) | Brand Name Cost** | Generic Cost*** | Generic Name | Generic Savings |
| Adderall XR 20mg | 30 | $215.83 | $148.50 | Amphetamine Mixture | $67.33 |
| Ambien 10mg | 30 | $172.76 | $3.00 | Zolpidem Tartrate | $169.76 |
| Klonopin 0.5mg | 60 | $90.73 | $4.20 | Clonazepam | $86.53 |
| Paxil CR 25mg | 30 | $119.95 | $80.21 | Paroxetine HCl | $39.74 |
| Risperdal 1mg | 60 | $320.11 | $204.75 | Risperidone | $115.36 |
| Ritalin 10mg | 90 | $96.59 | $16.20 | Methylpheni- date HCl | $80.39 |
| Valium 5mg | 60 | $187.55 | $1.82 | Diazepam | $185.73 |
| Wellbutrin XL 300mg | 30 | $221.18 | $45.00 | Bupropion HCl | $176.18 |
| Xanax 0.5mg | 90 | $143.69 | $4.50 | Alprazolam | $139.19 |
| Zoloft 100mg | 30 | $115.97 | $7.50 | Sertraline HCl | $108.47 |

* Most common strength dispensed for Blue Cross/Blue Shield of Michigan members.
** Brand-name cost based on Average Wholesale Price (AWP) obtained from various data sources (October 2009).
*** Generic cost based on Blue Cross/Blue Shield of Michigan Maximum Allowable Cost (MAC) schedule or discounted AWP (October 2009).
Source: Blue Cross Blue Shield of Michigan. "Brand-Name vs. Generic Drug Costs." Available online. URL: http://www.bcbsm.com/pdf/ps_generic.pdf. Accessed on September 14, 2009.

had to join the program to be able to collect his or her fee. The fees were considerably reduced from what used to be paid out for the same services. Many policies did not include "out-of-network" coverage, so if a patient went to a practitioner who was not in the plan, the fee came out of the individual's pocket. Today, many practitioners join the networks and attempt to make up the difference by treating a larger number of patients who are all members of the plan.

A similar situation exists in relation to the medicines prescribed. If an insurance plan includes coverage for pharmaceuticals, participating pharmacies must accept less than they used to for medicines dispensed. Once again, they attempt to make up the difference by dispensing medications to more customers.

## DRUG ABUSE ASSOCIATED WITH ANTIANXIETY PRESCRIPTION MEDICATIONS

When considering the costs of therapy and medication, one more area cannot be ignored. That is, the extent and costs associated with abuse of antianxiety medications. Although antianxiety medications may not bring about a physical addiction, psychological addiction is not uncommon.[12] Generally, when antianxiety drugs are used to treat genuine anxiety disorders, they are often

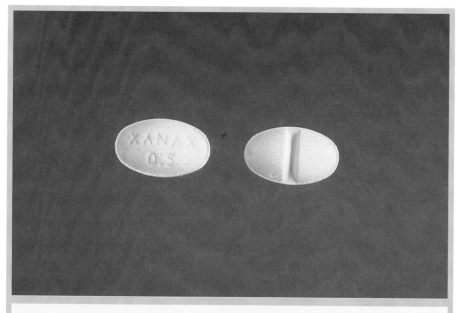

**Figure 6.1** Xanax, a common antianxiety medication, is sometimes abused and comes with a high risk of addiction. *(Drug Enforcement Administration)*

prescribed on a short-term basis. Unfortunately, addiction is not uncommon and, once the prescription runs out and the doctor is unwilling to write another one, individuals often seek illegal sources of these medications. Long-term use of antianxiety medications will lead to serious harm.

Additionally, if the user wishes to stop taking these medications, serious withdrawal symptoms develop, including more anxiety, insomnia, irritability, convulsions, nausea, hallucinations, and delirium. In these cases, further treatment with legitimate prescriptions and possible hospitalization are required. All of this places a tremendous financial burden on those people who are abusing the drugs and on the health care system as a whole. The overall cost of substance abuse in the United States is approximately $484 billion per year: $185 billion due to alcohol abuse, $161 billion in illegal drug abuse, and $138 billion related to smoking. In comparison, the annual cost for treating diabetes is approximately $131.7 billion and that for treating cancer is $171.6 billion.[13]

Central nervous system depressants such as the benzodiazepines (Valium, Librium, Xanax) and barbiturates (phenobarbital, pentobarbital, secobarbital) may be abused, taken orally or crushed and snorted.

Stimulants (Ritalin, Dexedrine) may be taken orally, crushed and snorted, or liquefied and injected into a vein. Some abusers also introduce these drugs anally.

Generally, abuse of antidepressants is not extremely common in the general population. Of course, any drug may be abused if it is overused, but if excessive use doesn't bring about the desired result, an individual will not continue to overuse the drug.

## WHERE TO GO FOR TREATMENT

Once an individual feels that he or she is suffering from anxiety or depression, or when family, friends, or coworkers observe a change in behavior consistent with these conditions, getting help quickly is of the utmost importance. A student in primary or secondary school can begin by visiting a school nurse. College students can go to the college's health service office to discuss the problem. Outside of these settings, individuals should first see their family doctor who might feel competent to treat them medically, or refer them to a qualified psychiatric health professional.

If a person does not have a family physician or health insurance coverage, state health departments provide free or low-cost mental health clinics where he or she can receive care for a problem.

Many large corporations also provide basic health care services to their employees. If anxiety or depression seems to be interfering with a person's ability to perform his or her job, health care professionals at the worksite will examine and direct the worker toward proper care to treat the condition. No matter where the problem exists, time is of the essence to ensure a recovery.

# 7

# Trends in Research and Drug Development

*Walter had suffered with depression for many years. During that time, he sought help from one psychiatrist after another. Each one would prescribe one or more medications designed to help him, but he just didn't get any long-term relief. At times, Walter's condition improved somewhat, but he was never truly free from his depressive episodes. He felt frustrated and lost. His main concern was that he would never be rid of the condition and his life would not be worth living.*

*One day, Walter was browsing the Web and came across information that gave him some hope. There were several research studies that were designed to develop new medications and combinations of medications to treat major depressive disorder in patients who had not responded to conventional treatments. Perhaps, Walter thought, relief might be within his grasp.*

## NEW MEDICATION APPROVAL

Walter felt encouraged when he read that several research studies were being conducted that were aimed at getting new antidepressants approved by the Food and Drug Administration (FDA). It is this branch of the U.S. Department of Health and Human Services that is responsible for approving the sale of new medications, medical and radiological devices, food and cosmetics, biologics, and veterinary drugs.

More specifically, the Center for Drug Evaluation and Research (CDER) is the branch of the FDA that ensures a drug is safe and effective.[1] While they don't actually test each drug, CDER's Office of Testing and Research conducts limited research in the areas of drug quality, safety, and effectiveness. It is the largest of the FDA's five centers and is responsible for both prescription and over-the-counter medications.

When a pharmaceutical company wants to get a new drug approved, it must perform rigorous tests and prove that the drug is safe and effective. The company must file an Investigational New Drug (IND) application to CDER. This is done after preliminary research in the laboratory yields promising results. The application is reviewed by CDER's chemists, statisticians, physicians, pharmacologists, and various other scientists. The application must contain information on animal pharmacology and toxicology studies, manufacturing information, clinical protocols, and investigator information.

When the IND is approved, clinical trials may begin. These use human subjects to determine safety, efficacy, and what side effects might occur. Strict regulations and guidelines must be adhered to during this phase of testing. Once the manufacturer is satisfied that there is enough evidence about the drug's safety and effectiveness to meet FDA guidelines, a New Drug Application (NDA) is submitted. The NDA includes full information on manufacturing specifications, method of analysis of each dosage form that is intended to be marketed, manufacturing specifications, packaging and labeling for both consumers and physicians, and the results of any new toxicological studies that have been performed since the IND application was submitted. If everything submitted is satisfactory to the CDER panel, the drug will be approved for marketing.

## CURRENT DRUG RESEARCH

Many research projects are underway to find new medications to treat anxiety and depression.[2] These projects include the development of new drugs as well as the use of older medications in combination with each other.

One such study involves the development of triple reuptake inhibitors or **serotonin-norepinephrine dopamine inhibitors (SNDRIs)**. Unlike SSRIs and SNRIs, these drugs also inhibit dopamine reuptake.[3] One of the researchers deeply involved in this avenue of development is Dr. Elliott Richelson at the Mayo Clinic. He refers to these drugs as "broad spectrum" antidepressants. They are hypothesized to have a more rapid onset of action and better efficacy than the older SSRIs and SNRIs.[4]

Another drug being studied is Viladozone.[5] Recently, the drug proved successful in the second of two Phase 3 clinical trials. Phase 3 trials are the last stage in the research process required by the FDA before it can consider a drug for approval. Viladozone is a unique SSRI in that it not only blocks reuptake of serotonin, but it also acts as a partial agonist of the 5-1a receptor. An agonist is a chemical substance that acts on a receptor to initiate the same reaction as that produced by a naturally occurring substance. Thus, this drug not only increases the amount of serotonin in the synapse by blocking its reuptake, but it also stimulates the receptor as if it were an additional dose of serotonin. In addition, this drug does not display the sexual side effects of causing or worsening sexual dysfunction as seen with other SSRIs.

A different approach to treating depression is the use of the veterinary anesthetic ketamine.[6] This drug acts as an N-methyl d-aspartate (NMDA) antagonist. NMDA is an amino acid derivative that is an agonist at the NMDA receptor and mimics the excitatory neurotransmitter glutamate. It appears that NMDA antagonists enhance the antidepressant effects of α-amino-3-hydroxyl-5-methyl-4-isoxazole-propionate (AMPA), which also mimics the actions of glutamate. An excitatory neurotransmitter may act to stimulate the individual and help him or her to overcome a depressive episode. In addition, ketamine's effects were strong, rapid, and lasted longer than other NMDA antagonists.

Another approach to treating anxiety and depression involves the combining of older drugs that were initially used independently. A research study was underway at the Chang Gung Memorial Hospital in Taiwan to determine whether Quetiapine, a drug originally approved by the FDA in 1997 to treat schizophrenia and in 2004 to treat bipolar disorder, will improve the efficacy of SSRIs or SNRIs in the treatment of primary anxiety disorder or mood disorders accompanied by anxiety symptoms.[7] The study was expected to be completed by the end of 2010.

New drugs are also being investigated to treat anxiety with particular emphasis on medications that cause minimal side effects. Dr. Rainer Rupprecht and his team at the Max Planck Institute of Psychiatry in Munich, Germany, are studying the effects of an antianxiety medication based on neurosteroids derived from the hormone progesterone.[8]

Neurosteroids are synthesized in the central and peripheral nervous systems and alter nerve excitability. The substance that Dr. Rupprecht's team is investigating is called XBD173 and it was shown that this chemical stimulated the synthesis of neurosteroids. The study was designed to test whether an increase in neurosteroid production could alleviate the symptoms of anxiety effectively and, at the same time, avoid bringing about the usual side effects that accompany traditional antianxiety medications.

A clinical trial was carried out using 70 healthy volunteer subjects. The participants were injected with a chemical (CCK-4) that triggered a short anxiety and panic attack that lasted two to five minutes. The next step was to administer XBD173 and again inject CCK-4. This time, no panic attacks occurred. After this, the subjects were given the benzodiazepine Alprazolam and the CCK-4 and, once again, no panic attack ensued. However, all of the participants reported that they experienced fatigue when they took the drug and withdrawal symptoms when it was stopped. Only mild gastrointestinal problems were experienced when the XBD173 was administered. Because Dr. Rupprecht is unsure that XBD173 will work on a real panic attack, additional clinical trials will be carried out.

## ADDITIONAL CLINICAL TRIALS

Clinical trials are typically conducted using individuals who are suffering from the condition for which the medication under investigation is being used or is intended to be used. However, in some trials healthy individuals are the test subjects. In most cases, this is done to determine possible side effects of a medication or just to see how the medication affects people in general.

### Alprazolam

One such trial involves an investigation as to whether a new sublingual form of alprazolam (Xanax) will have the same level of bioavailability as the currently used immediate release tablet. The Pfizer pharmaceutical company is sponsoring this research.[9]

Another study is aimed at determining whether a generic form of alprazolam that will be sold in Brazil has the same efficacy as brand name alprazolam sold in the United States.[10] Once again, healthy test subjects will be recruited for this investigation.

## Bupropion

Some clinical studies are designed to determine not only how a drug directly affects the condition that it is designed to treat, but also how other aspects of a patient's functions are affected. In a clinical trial being conducted at Queen's University in Kingston, Ontario, Canada, the effects on sleep patterns in patients with major depressive disorder are being tested based on the use of different forms of Wellbutrin.[11]

The study is designed to determine if there is a difference in the effects on sleeping patterns when a patient uses Wellbutrin SR, a sustained release form of the drug or Wellbutrin XL, an extended release form of the medication.

In another clinical trial involving bupropion, two different factors are being tested. The first is the bioavailability of the drug under fasting conditions. The second is whether a generic form of the drug has the same bioavailability under these fasting conditions as the brand name medication.[12] In this study, researchers are looking for test subjects who are suffering with any depressive disorder. The drugs are being tested in the fasting state so that absorption is not impeded by the presence of food.

## Clonazepam

Clinical trials of Clonazepam (Klonopin) are underway in several different areas. One study being conducted by the National Institute of Mental Health involves the use of several drugs that treat social anxiety disorder.[13] In this trial, the study will compare the effectiveness of either adding clonazepam or placebo to standard treatment or switching to venlafaxine (Effexor) in treating generalized social anxiety disorder in individuals who have not responded to treatment with sertraline (Zoloft).

Three different experimental groups will be studied. The first will take both sertraline and clonazepam, the second will take venlafaxine only, and the third will take both sertraline and a placebo. Many different types of results will be studied and interpreted such as effectiveness of the treatment, side effects, patient compliance, and others.

## Venlafaxine

Depression may result from any number of factors, including marijuana use. A clinical trial addressing this issue is underway.[14] Sponsored by the National

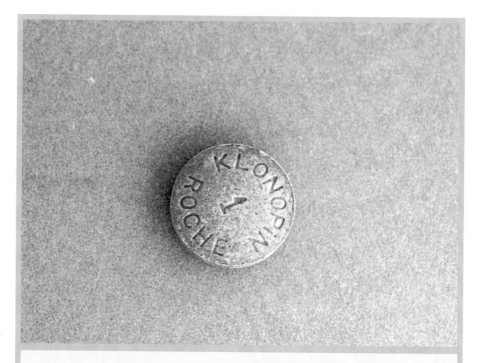

**Figure 7.1** Clonazepam (brand name Klonopin) is being studied in clinical trials for effectiveness of use in combination with sertraline, an antidepressant. (© *Custom Medical Stock Photo*)

Institute on Drug Abuse, researchers in this study are attempting to determine if venlafaxine (Effexor) extended release tablets are effective in treating individuals with marijuana addiction and depression. Participants will receive either the medication (375 mg per day) or a placebo and will be tested twice each week through urine samples to screen for drugs. In addition to the medication or the placebo, each participant will receive individualized psychotherapy sessions. Healthy subjects will not be included in this study.[14]

Another clinical trial of venlafaxine is being conducted by the Max Planck Institute of Psychiatry in Munich, Germany. In this study, venlafaxine is being used to augment treatment with quetiapine (Seroquel) which is used to treat bipolar depression and anxiety disorders. The goal is to determine whether the addition of venlafaxine to treatment with quetiapine will be effective in treating depression that is treatment resistant. Once again, one group will get

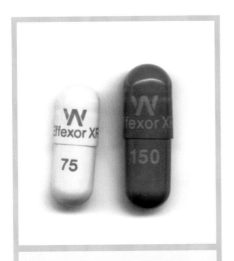

**Figure 7.2** Venlafaxine (brand name Effexor) is being studied for effectiveness in treating patients with both depression and marijuana addiction. *(Photo by Parhamr)*

the test drug quetiapine in conjunction with the true drug of augmentation venlafaxine and the other group will get a combination of quetiapine and a placebo. Unlike some of the other trials, healthy subjects will not be included.[15]

## Memantine

This drug, marketed under several trade names (Abixa, Akatinol, Axura, Ebia, and Namenda) is used to treat Alzheimer's disease. Memantine is being tested as a treatment for a number of different conditions including generalized anxiety disorder. It acts as an antagonist at the $5HT_3$ receptor, which attaches to serotonin in the brain.

A clinical trial is currently being conducted by Upstate Medical University of the State University of New York to determine the effectiveness of using memantine in conjunction with SSRIs or SNRIs to treat persistent anxiety. Participants must be suffering with either generalized anxiety disorder or social anxiety disorder and must be only partial responders to treatment with SSRIs or SNRIs. In addition, the study will determine whether the drug combination will also improve sleep quality.[16]

## Experimental Drugs

Each of the clinical trials above involves the use of drugs that are already on the market. Clinical trials are also being conducted with new, experimental drugs so that enough clinical data is collected to convince the FDA that approval is warranted.

One such study is being sponsored by the National Institute of Mental Health. An experimental drug known as AZD2327 is being tested to determine whether it can effectively treat depression and anxiety. The drug, which has been tested in animals and humans, has shown that it causes changes in certain body chemicals that may make it effective. Studies have also shown that the drug is an enkephalinergic agonist, a substance that activates receptors for the brain neurotransmitter enkephalin. Enkephalin has opiate qualities and it appears that this approach may be very effective in treating both anxiety and depression.[17]

Another clinical trial is being conducted by Dr. Jonathan Henry at Michigan State University on a drug called F2695 SR, which is designed to treat depression by normalizing serotonin and norepinephrine while reducing two common side effects of antidepressants: headache and nausea. It is hoped that, although it works similarly to other drugs in its class that have previously been approved, it will be more effective and more tolerable.[18]

Experimental drugs are not the only substances being tested to treat depression and anxiety. Another clinical trial is being conducted by the National Center for Complementary and Alternative Medicine (NCCAM). In this study, chamomile (*Matricaria recutita*) extract is being tested to determine how effective it is in treating general anxiety disorder (GAD). This is based on the fact that chamomile has traditionally been used as a calmative and is well tolerated. This trial is being done to further research already performed in an earlier trial that showed promising results. The researchers are hoping that the chamomile helps to prevent relapses in patients who have recovered from GAD.[19]

At times, drugs that are totally unrelated to antidepressants and antianxiety drugs may be effective in treating depression and anxiety. In another clinical trial, the antibiotic d-cycloserine (DSC) is being tested as an enhancer to treat social phobia. In this study, researchers are attempting to determine whether the antibiotic may be used to boost the effectiveness of cognitive behavioral therapy (CBT).[20]

Although CBT is effective in treating social anxiety disorder, about 40% of those treated continue to have symptoms. The antibiotic has been shown to enhance the type of learning promoted by CBT therapy. Again, the study will utilize both the drug to be tested and a placebo.

In a slightly different clinical trial, the same antibiotic and the same form of psychotherapy are being tested, but this time as a treatment for panic disorder. Previous animal studies showed that d-cycloserine was able to enhance extinction of phobias.[21]

# IN SUMMARY

Anxiety and depression may exist as individual conditions or they may occur simultaneously. How an individual presents him or herself depends on many factors including genetics, social environment, general health of the patient, and socioeconomic conditions.

Medications for the treatment of anxiety and depression have come a long way over the past several decades. Laboratories used to synthesize compounds and test their efficacy have evolved from simple rooms with minimal equipment to modern, complex structures with advanced synthesizing and testing equipment.

The need for efficacious antianxiety and antidepressant medications continues to increase as more and more people suffer from these afflictions. The economic costs associated with treating these conditions continue to skyrocket, putting a great burden on the health care system, insurance companies, and families. The social impact related to the growing number of individuals with anxiety and depression is also becoming more serious as divorce rates rise, the unemployment rate related to the inability to perform a job increases, and many interpersonal relationships deteriorate.

Scientists are continuing to increase their understanding of why anxiety and depression occur and which medications may be used to treat these conditions effectively. As technology advances, newer forms of older medications are being created and new families of drugs are being discovered in an effort to treat the millions of people worldwide suffering with these afflictions. There is hope, even if it takes time, as progress is made in the pharmacological and psychotherapeutic treatments of anxiety and depression. As difficult as it may be for the sufferers and those close to them, patience will pay off in the end.

# Notes

## Chapter 1

1. Mark H. Pollack, "Generalized Anxiety Disorder—Overview and Case History," Medscape, http://www.medscape.com/viewarticle/527758_1 (posted on March 28, 2006).

2. Jeanie Lerche Davis, "Is It Really Depression? Symptoms of Depression, Anxiety Disorder and Bipolar Disorder Have Similarities—But Require Different Treatments," WebMD, http://www.webmd.com/anxiety-panic/guide/is-really-depression (posted on February 3, 2006).

3. *Anxiety Disorders Association of America, "Generalized Anxiety Disorder (GAD)," http://www.adaa.org/AboutADAA/Press Room/Stats&Facts.asp (accessed on February 28, 2009).*

4. Anxiety Disorders Association of America, "Statistics and Facts About Anxiety Disorders," http://www.adaa.org/AboutADAA/PressRoom/Stats&Facts.asp (accessed on March 5, 2009).

5. Medical Breakthroughs, "Anxiety's Hidden Costs," June 25, 2009, http://www.ivanhoe.com/channels/p_printStory.cfm?storyid=21759 (accessed on July 13, 2009).

6. Eric Wilinski, "The Economic Costs of Anxiety," Panic! A Blog About Panic, Anxiety, Depression and Related Topics, July 26, 2007, http://panicanddepression.blogspot.com/2007/07/economic-costs-of-anxiety_26.html (accessed on July 21, 2009).

7. Kathleen Kingsbury, "Tallying Mental Illness' Costs," *Time,* May 9, 2008, http://www.time.com/time/health/article/0,8599,1738804,00.html (accessed March 5, 2009).

8. Laura Pratt and Debra Brody, "Depression in the United States Household Population, 2005–2006," NCHS Data Brief, http://www.cdc.gov/NCHS/data/databriefs/db07.htm (posted September 2008).

9. "Causes of Depression," WebMD, http://www.webmd.com/depression/guide/

causes-depression (accessed on May 7, 2009).

10. MedicineNet.com, "Generalized Anxiety Disorder (GAD)," http://www.medicinenet.com/anxiety/article.htm#tocd (accessed on March 8, 2010).

11. National Institute of Mental Health, "Mental Health Medications," http://www.nimh.nih.gov/health/publications/mental-health-medications/complete-index.shtml#pub2. Accessed on March 8, 2010.

## Chapter 2

1. Joseph A. Lieberman, "History of the Use of Antidepressants in Primary Care," *Primary Care Companion Journal of Clinical Psychiatry* 5, suppl. 7 (2003): 6–10.

2. G. E. Crane, "The Psychiatric Side-Effects of Iproniazid," *American Journal of Psychiatry* 112 (1956): 494–501.

3. Myrna Weissman, "Treatment of Depression: Bridging the 21st Century," (Washington, DC: American Psychopathological Association, 2001), 10–11.

4. N. S. Kline, "Chemical Experience with Iproniazid (Marsilid)," *Journal of Clinical Experimental Psychopharmacology* 19 (1961): 72–78.

5. R. W. Fuller, K. W. Perry, and B. B. Molloy, "Effect of an Update Inhibitor on Serotonin Metabolism in Rat Brain: Studies with 3-(p-trifluoromethylphenoxy)-N-methyl-3-phenylopropylamine (Lilly 110140)," *Life Science* 15 (1974), 1161–1171.

6. See note 1 above.

7. Tony Dokoupil, "How Mother Found Her Helper: The Story of America's Long Infatuation with Anti-anxiety Drugs," *Newsweek,* January 22, 2009, http://www.newsweek.com/id/180998 (accessed on May 27, 2009).

8. L. Saxon, P. Hjemdahl, A. J. Hiltunen, and S. Borg. "Effects of Flumazenil in the Treatment of Benzodiazepine Withdrawal—A Double-blind Pilot Study," *Psychopharmacology,* 131, no. 2 (May 1997), 153–160; C. Bismuth, M. Le Bellec, S. Dally, and G. Lagier. "[Benzodiazepine physical dependence. 6 cases ]," *La Nouvelle Presse Médicale* 9, no. 28 (June 28, 1980): 1941–1945.

## Chapter 3

1. National Institute of Mental Health, "Key Molecule in Inflammation-Related Depression Confirmed," March 20, 2009, http://www.nimh.nih.

gov/science-news/2009/
key-molecule-in-inflammation-
related-depression-confirmed.
shtml (accessed on June 9,
2009).

2. Ted Dinan, "Physical Consequences of Depression," *The
Irish Scientist,* http://www.
irishscientist.ie/2000/contents.
asp?contentxml=084bs.
xml&contentxsl=insight3.xsl
(accessed June 9, 2009).

3. Jogin H. Thakore, et al.,
"Increased Intraabdominal Fat
Deposition in Patients with
Major Depressive Illness as
Measured by Computed Tomo-
graphy," *Biological Psychiatry,* 41
(June 1, 1997): 1140–1142.

4. Jogin H. Thakore (ed). *Physical Consequences of Depression*
(Petersfield, U.K.: Wrightson
Biomedical Publishing, 2001)
239.

5. Medical News Today, "New
Survey Finds Financial Consequences of Depression are
Seventy-Five Percent Higher
Among Floridians Than the
National Average," July 14,
2006, http://www.medical
newstoday.com/articles/47039.
php (accessed on June 10,
2009).

6. Andrew Mackinnon, Anthony
Jorm, and Ian Hickie, "A
National Depression Index for
Australia," *The Medical Jour-*
*nal of Australia* 181, suppl. 7
(October 4, 2004), S52–S56,
http://www.mja.com.au/
public/issues/181_07_041004/
mac10800_fm.html (accessed
on June 11, 2009).

7. National Center for PTSD Fact-
Sheet, "What is Post Traumatic
Stress Disorder (PTSD)?" http://
www.ncptsd.va.gov/ncmain/
ncdocs/fact_shts/fs_what_is_
ptsd.html (accessed on June 4,
2009).

8. National Institute of Mental Health, "Post-Traumatic
Stress Disorder (PTSD),"
http://www.nimh.nih.gov/
health/publications/post-
traumatic-stress-disorder-
ptsd/nimh_ptsd_booklet.pdf
(accessed on April 30, 2009).

9. Jonas Donner, et. al., "An
Association Analysis of Murine
Anxiety Genes in Humans
Implicates Novel Candidate
Genes for Anxiety Disorders,"
*Biological Psychiatry,* 64, no. 8
(October 15, 2008), p. 672–680,
http://www.sciencedaily.com/
releases/2008/08/080827100818.
htm (accessed on June 8, 2009).

10. American Psychiatric Association, "Anxiety Disorders,"
in *Diagnostic and Statistical
Manual of Mental Disorders.* 4th
ed. Text rev. (Washington, DC:
American Psychiatric Association, 2000), 429–441.

11. Peter H. Silverstone and Mahnaz Salsali, "Low Self-esteem and Psychiatric Patients: Part I—The Relationship Between Low Self-esteem and Psychiatric Diagnosis," *Annals of General Hospital Psychiatry* 2, no. 2 (February 11, 2003), http://www.annals-general-psychiatry.com/content/2/1/2#IDATL4ZE (accessed on June 4, 2009).

12. Harvard Health Publications, "Can Life Experiences Cause Anxiety Disorders?" August 27, 2007, http://www.gather.com/viewArticle.action?articleId=281474977098905 (accessed on June 8, 2009).

## Chapter 4

1. Eric H. Chudler, "Brain Facts and Figures," University of Washington, Seattle, http://faculty.washington.edu/chudler/facts.html (accessed on June 16, 2009).

2. Maj-Britt Niemi, "Placebo Effect: A cure in the Mind." *Scientific American Mind*," pp. 42–49, February 2009, http://www.scientificamerican.com/article.cfm?id=placebo-effect-a-cure-in-the-mind (accessed on July 7, 2010).

3. Rick Nauert, "Placebo Effect Among Antidepressants." *PsychCentral*, August 16, 2007, http://psychcentral.com/news/2007/08/15/placebo-effect-among-antidepressants/1131.html.

4. BBC News, "Dummy drugs 'can relieve anxiety.'" *BBC News*, June 18, 2005. Available online. URL: http://news.bbc.co.uk/2/hi/health/4095498.stm.

5. Barbara K. Hecht and Frederick Hecht, "Antidepressants and Suicide, FDA Warns," *MedicineNet.com*, March 2004, http://www.medicinenet.com/script/main/art.asp?articlekey=31649 (accessed on July 8, 2010).

6. U.S. Food and Drug Administration, "Revisions to Product Labeling," http://www.fda.gov/downloads/Drugs/DrugSafety/InformationbyDrugClass/UCM173233.pdf (accessed July 8, 2010).

7. Gustav Drasch, et al., "Frequency of Different Antidepressants Associated with Suicides and Drug Deaths," *International Journal of Legal Medicine*, volume 122 (2), pp. 115–121, March 2008, http://www.springerlink.com/content/c27m7720k53h788q/ (accessed on July 8, 2010).

## Chapter 5

1. Science Daily, "New Generation of Rapid-Acting Antidepressants?" March 6, 2010,

http://www.sciencedaily. com/releases/2010/03/ 100301111407.htm (accessed March 10, 2010).

2. A. C. Butler, J. E. Chapman, E. M. Forman and A. T. Beck, "The Empirical Status of Cognitive-Behavioral Therapy: A Review of Meta-analyses," *ClinicalPsychology Review.* 26, no. 1 (January 26, 2006), 17–31.

3. René F. Marineau, "Ancestors and Family: The Birth of a Myth," *Jacob Levy Moreno, 1889–1974: Father of Psychodrama, Sociometry, and Group Psychotherapy* (New York: Routledge, 1989), 4–6.

4. Louise B. Andrew, "Depression and Suicide: Treatment and Medication," emedicine from WebMD, June 23, 2008. http://emedicine.medscape. com/article/805459-treatment (accessed on July 27, 2009).

5. MGH Hotline Online, "Electroconvulsive Therapy Discussion Hosted at the MGH," Massachusetts General Hospital Publication for Employees and Staff, October 13, 2006, http://www2. massgeneral.org/pubaffairs/ issues2006/101306ect.htm (accessed on July 27, 2009).

6. W. Vaughn McCall, et al., "Health-Related Quality of Life Following ECT in a Large Community Sample," *Journal of*

*Affective Disorders* 90, no. 2–3 (February 2006): pp. 269–274.

7. Lemeneh Tefera and Lauren Tomeo, "Anxiety: Treatment and Medication," emedicine from WebMD, November 20, 2008, http://emedicine.medscape. com/article/805265-treatment (accessed on July 30, 2009).

8. J. Levine, "Controlled Trials of Inositol in Psychiatry," *European Psychopharmacology,* 7, no. 2 (May 1997), 147–155.

9. University of Maryland Medical Center, "Omega-3 Fatty Acids," http://www.umm. edu/altmed/articles/omega-3–000316.htm (accessed on September 4, 2009).

10. C. Maurizi, "The Therapeutic Potential for Tryptophan and Melatonin: Possible Roles in Depression, Sleep, Alzheimer's Disease and Abnormal Aging," *Medical Hypotheses,* 31 (1990): 233–242.

11. Mayo Foundation for Medical Education and Research, "Ginkgo (Ginkgo biloba L.)," MayoClinic.com, http://www. mayoclinic.com/health/ginkgo-biloba/NS_patient-ginkgo (accessed on September 8, 2009).

12. Juniper Russo, "Natural Antidepressants Compared: Examining Fish Oil, Kanna, SAM-e and St. John's Wort," February 24, 2009, http://natural

medicine.suite101.com/article.
cfm/natural_antidepressants_
compared (accessed on September 8, 2009).

13. Ibid.

14. Shannon Bindler and Margalit
Ward, "10 Natural Antidepressants to Boost Your Spirits," *The
Huffington Post,* July 15, 2009,
http://www.huffingtonpost.com/
shannon-bindler/10-natural-
antidepressant_b_232506.html
(accessed May 14, 2010).

15. Kimberly Pryor, "Stress and
Anxiety: Natural Support
to Calm Anxious Nerves,"
http://www.vrp.com/articles.
aspx?ProdID=1811 (accessed
on September 8, 2009).

16. Uncommon Knowledge, Ltd.,
"Depression Learning Path,"
Depression: Understand It,
Treat It, Beat It, http://www.
clinical-depression.co.uk/
depression-learning-path/
(accessed on May 14, 2010).

## Chapter 6

1. Laura A. Pratt and Debra J.
Brody, "Depression in the
United States Household Population, 2005–2006," National
Center for Health Statistics,
Centers for Disease Control
and Prevention, September
2008, http://www.cdc.gov/
nchs/data/databriefs/db07.htm
(accessed September 10, 2009).

2. A.D. Lopez and C. Murray,
"The Global Burden of Disease,
1990–2020," *Nature Medicine*
4, no. 11 (November 1998),
1241–1243.

3. Canadian Mental Health
Association, "Effects of Depression and Anxiety on Canadian
Society," http://www.cmha.ca/
bins/print_page.asp?cid=5-34-
183&lang=1 (accessed September 10, 2009).

4. J. Unutzer, et al., "Health Care
Costs Associated with Depression in Medically Ill Fee-for-
Service Medicare Participants,"
*Journal of the American Geri-
atric Society* 57, no. 3 (March
2009), 506–510.

5. Ibid.

6. EMedTV, "Depression Statistics," http://depression.emedtv.
com/depression/depression-
statistics.html (accessed May 11,
2010).

7. American Academy of Child
and Adolescent Psychiatry,
"Teen Suicide," http://www.
aacap.org/cs/root/facts_for_
families/teen_suicide (accessed
September 14, 2009).

8. Anxiety Disorders Association of America, "Statistics and
Facts About Anxiety Disorders,"
http://www.adaa.org/About
ADAA/PressRoom/Stats&Facts.
asp (accessed September 14,
2009).

9. Consumer Reports, "Anti-depressants: Summary of Recommendations," July 2009, http://www.consumerreports. org/health/resources/pdf/best-buy-drugs/Antidepressants_ update.pdf (accessed September 14, 2009).

10. Blue Cross Blue Shield of Michigan, "Generic Drugs," http://www.bcbsm.com/ member/prescription_drugs/ generic_drugs.shtml (accessed September 14, 2009).

11. Jim Hutt, "How Much Does Counseling Cost?" Counselor Link, http://www.counselorlink. com/faqs/cost-of-counseling/ (accessed September 14, 2009).

12. Steps2rehab, "Anti-Anxiety Drugs," http://www.steps2rehab. com/addictions/prescription-drugs/anti-anxiety-drugs/ (accessed September 15, 2009).

13. National Institute of Drug Abuse (NIDA), "Drug Abuse Is Costly," January 2008 http:// www.drugabuse.gov/about/ welcome/aboutdrugabuse/ magnitude/, (accessed September 15, 2009).

## Chapter 7

1. U.S. Food and Drug Administration, "How Drugs Are Developed and Approved," http://www.fda.gov/Drugs/ DevelopmentApprovalProcess/ HowDrugsareDevelopedand Approved/default.htm (accessed September 16, 2009).

2. ClincialTrials.gov, "Open Studies/antidepressants," http:// clinicaltrials.gov/search/open/ intervention=antidepressants (accessed September 17, 2009); ClinicalTrials.gov, "Open Studies/anxiety," http:// clinicaltrials.gov/search/open/ intervention=%22anxiety%22 (accessed September 17, 2009).

3. Elliott Richelson, "Triple Reuptake Inhibitors as a New Generation of Antidepressant Drugs," *Journal of Affective Disorders,* 107, suppl. 1 (March 2008), p. S36.

4. Liang Yanqi and Elliott Richelson, "Triple Reuptake Inhibitors: Next-Generation Antidepressants," *Primary Psychiatry* 15, no. 4 (2008), 50–56, http://www.primarypsychiatry. com/aspx/articledetail.aspx? articleid=1525 (accessed on September 17, 2009).

5. Psych Central, "New Antidepressant, Viladozone, Shows Promise, No Sexual Side Effects," Psychcentral.com, June 2, 2009, http://psychcentral.com/ news/2009/06/02/new-antidepressant-viladozone-shows-promise-no-sexual-side-effects/6266.html (accessed on September 17, 2009).

6. Sungho Maeng, et al., "Cellular Mechanisms Underlying the Antidepressant Effects of Ketamine: Role of Alpha-amino-3-hydroxy-5-methyisoxazole-4-propionic Acid Receptors," Biological Psychiatry, 63, no. 4 (February 15, 2008), 347–348.

7. ClinicalTrials.gov, "Open Studies/anxiety," http://clinicaltrials.gov/search/open/intervention=%22anxiety%22 (accessed on September 17, 2009).

8. The China Post, "New Anti-anxiety Drug to Have Fewer Side Effects: German Scientists," August 11, 2009, http://chinapost.com.tw/health/mental-health/2009/08/11/219976/new-anti-anxiety.htm (accessed September 17, 2009).

9. National Institutes of Health, "Bioequivalence of a New Sublingual and a Reference Alprazolam Immediate Release Tablet Formulation," Clinical TrialsFeed.org, December 7, 2009, http://clinicaltrialsfeeds.org/clinical-trials/show/NCT01027689 (accessed March 11, 2010).

10. National Institutes of Health, "Bioequivalence of a Test Alprazolam Sublingual Formulation Compared to a Commercial Sublingual Formulation,"

ClinicalTrialsFeed.org, April 7, 2009, http://clinicaltrialsfeeds.org/clinical-trials/show/NCT00877955 (accessed March 11, 2010).

11. National Institutes of Health, "Does Sleep Quality Change After Switch from Wellbutrin SR to Wellbutrin XL in Patients With Major Depressive Disorder?" ClinicalTrialsFeed.org, February 10, 2009, http://clinicaltrialsfeeds.org/clinical-trials/show/NCT00616915 (accessed March 11, 2010).

12. National Institutes of Health, "Bupropion Hydrochloride 300 mg Extended Release Tablets Under Fasting Conditions," ClinicalTrialsFeed.org, January 8, 2010, http://clinicaltrialsfeeds.org/clinical-trials/show/NCT01046214 (accessed March 11, 2010).

13. National Institutes of Health, "Improving Treatment Outcomes in Pharmacotherapy of Generalized Social Anxiety Disorder," ClinicalTrialsFeed.org, March 12, 2009, http://clinicaltrialsfeeds.org/clinical-trials/show/NCT00282828 (accessed March 11, 2010).

14. National Institutes of Health, "Free Venlafaxine Treatment for Marijuana Addiction and Depression," ClinicalTrialsFeed.org, October 15, 2009, http://

clinicaltrialsfeeds.org/clinical-trials/show/NCT00131456 (accessed March 11, 2010).

15. National Institutes of Health, "Venlafaxine augmentation in Treatment Resistant Depression," ClinicalTrialsFeed.org, September 17, 2009, http://clinicaltrialsfeeds.org/clinical-trials/show/NCT00253266 (accessed March 11, 2010).

16. National Institutes of Health, "A 10 Week Open-Label Pilot Study to Evaluate the Effectiveness and Safety of Memantine (Namenda) as Augmentation Therapy in Patients With Generalized Anxiety Disorder." ClinicalTrialsFeed.org, December 16, 2008, http://clinical trialsfeeds.org/clinical-trials/show/NCT00411398 (accessed March 11, 2010).

17. National Institutes of Health, "AZD2327 to Treat Anxious Major Depression," ClinicalTrials.gov, December 30, 2009, http://www.clinicaltrials.gov/show/NCT00738270 (accessed March 11, 2010).

18. PhysOrg.com, "MSU Researcher Studies Effects of Experimental Depression Medication," December 2, 2009, http://www.physorg.com/news178999354.html. (accessed March 11, 2010).

19. National Center for Complementary and Alternative Medicine, "Long Term Chamomile Therapy for Anxiety," ClinicalTrials.gov, February 18, 2010, http://clinicaltrials.gov/ct2/show/study/NCT01072344?term=anxiety+disorders+[CONDITION]+AND+NIH+[STUDY-SPONSORS-CLASS]+NOT+NIMH+[ORGANIZATION-NAME]&rank=29 (accessed March 11, 2010).

20. National Institute of Mental Health, "Use of an Antibiotic as an Enhancer for the Treatment of Social Phobia," ClinicalTrials.gov, February 3, 2010, http://clinicaltrials.gov/ct2/show/NCT00128401?term=anxiety+disorders+[CONDITION]+AND+NIH+[STUDY-SPONSORS-CLASS]+NOT+NIMH+[ORGANIZATION-NAME]&rank=62 (accessed March 11, 2010).

21. National Institute of Mental Health, "Exposure, D-Cycloserine Enhancement, and Genetic Modulators in Panic Disorder," Clinical Trials.gov, November 17, 2008, http://clinicaltrials.gov/ct2/show/NCT00790868?term=anxiety+disorders+[CONDITION]+AND+NIH+[STUDY-SPONSORS-CLASS]+NOT+NIMH+[ORGANIZATION-NAME]&rank=71 (accessed March 12, 2010).

# Glossary

**amphetamines**    A group of drugs that acts as a central nervous system stimulator. These are used to treat depression and to control appetite when weight loss is desired as in cases of obesity.

**anxiety**    State of fear and apprehension caused by the anticipation of a real or imagined impending threat. The individual's physical and psychological functions are often impaired.

**benzodiazepines**    A group of psychotropic medications used to treat anxiety and convulsions. These may be used as muscle relaxants, hypnotics, and sedatives.

**bipolar disorder**    A psychological disorder that manifests as alternating periods of depression and mania. Periods of normal mood often separate these extremes of behavior.

**cortisol**    A corticosteroid hormone produced in the adrenal cortex (the outer region of the gland) often referred to as the "stress hormone." It is secreted in high concentrations during periods of stress and anxiety, causing an increase in blood pressure and blood glucose levels and is one of the body's natural anti-inflammatories.

**depression**    A state of general emotional withdrawal and feelings of hopelessness lasting for a longer than average period of time. This is often accompanied by loss of appetite, sleeplessness, and sadness.

**flight-or-fight response**    A stimulation of the sympathetic nervous system that prepares an individual to react to a potentially dangerous situation. The person will experience an increase in heart and respiratory rates, pupil dilation, increased blood pressure, inhibition of the digestive system, dilation of blood vessels to muscles, inhibition of tear and saliva production, and several other responses.

**generalized anxiety disorder (GAD)**    A condition associated with excessive and often uncontrollable worry over everyday occurrences. The level of distress is usually out of proportion to the actual importance of what the individual is concerned about.

**insomnia**    The chronic inability to fall asleep and remain asleep for sufficient periods of time. It is a symptom of some underlying cause and not a condition in itself. The result of chronic insomnia is impairment of physical function and behavioral changes.

**lithium**    A metal with an atomic number of three that, in its citrate or carbonate form, is used to treat mania and bipolar disorder.

**monoamine oxidase inhibitors (MAOIs)**    A class of drugs that inhibits the action of the enzyme monoamine oxidase. This enzyme is used in the brain to break down monoamine neurotransmitters. These drugs are prescribed for cases of severe depression.

**neurotransmitter**    Any chemical substance that enables the transmission of a nerve impulse across the synaptic space between two neurons or from a neuron to a muscle or gland.

**post-partum depression**    Depression seen in 8–20% of women immediately following delivery of a baby. The cause is directly related to the rapid drop in estrogen and progesterone levels that have an effect on brain chemistry. It may occur right after delivery, or as much as one year later.

**selective serotonin reuptake inhibitors (SSRIs)**    A group of drugs that inhibits the reuptake of the neurotransmitter serotonin in the synapses of the brain, thus allowing it to remain for an extended period of time. This leads to modifications in behavior.

**serotonin-norepinephrine dopamine inhibitors (SNDRIs)**    A new class of drugs that inhibits the reuptake of serotonin, norepinephrine, and dopamine in the synapses of the brain. It is believed that this class of drugs will become the drugs of choice in treating anxiety and depression.

**serotonin-norepinephrine reuptake inhibitors (SNRIs)**    A group of drugs that inhibits the reuptake of the neurotransmitters serotonin and norepinephrine in the synapses of the brain. This will bring about a more extensive change in behavior than that seen with SSRIs.

**tricyclic antidepressants (TCAs)**    A group of medications that structurally contains three fused benzene rings used to treat depression and cocaine abuse.

# further Resources

Amen, Daniel G., and Lisa C. Routh. *Healing Anxiety and Depression.* New York: Penguin Group, 2003.

Beck, Aaron T., Gary Emery, and Ruth L. Greenberg. *Anxiety Disorders and Phobias: A Cognitive Perspective.* Cambridge, Mass.: Perseus Books Group, 2005.

Bourne, Edmund J. *The Anxiety and Phobia Workbook.* Oakland, Calif.: New Harbinger Publications, 2005.

Callahan, Christopher M., and German E. Berrios. *Reinventing Depression: A History of the Treatment of Depression in Primary Care, 1940–2004.* New York: Oxford University Press, 2005.

Craske, Michelle G., and David H. Barlow. *Mastery of your Anxiety and Worry.* New York: Oxford University Press, 2006.

Foa, Edna B., and Linda W. Andrews. *If Your Adolescent Has an Anxiety Disorder: An Essential Resource for Parents.* New York: Oxford University Press, 2006.

Goodwin, Fredrick K., and Kaye Redfield Jamison. *Manic-Depressive Illness: Bipolar Disorders and Recurrent Depression.* 2d ed. New York: Oxford University Press, 2007.

Gordon, James S. *Unstuck: Your Guide to the Seven-Stage Journey out of Depression.* London: Penguin Books, 2009.

Hope, Debra A., Richard Heimberg, and Cynthia L. Turk. *Managing Social Anxiety: A Cognitive Behavioral Therapy Approach.* New York: Oxford University Press, 2006.

Jongsma, Arthur E., Jr., ed. *The Complete Anxiety Treatment and Homework Planner.* Hoboken, N.J.: Wiley and Sons, 2004.

Martin, G. Neil. *Psychology: A Beginners Guide.* Oxford, U.K.: Oneworld Publications, 2008

Merrell, Kenneth W. *Helping Students Overcome Depression and Anxiety: A Practical Guide.* New York: The Guilford Press, 2008.

O'Connor, Richard. *Undoing Perpetual Stress: The Missing Connection Between Depression, Anxiety and 21st Century Illness.* New York: Penguin Group, 2006.

Peurifoy, Reneau Z. *Anxiety, Phobias and Panic: A Step-by-Step Program for Regaining Control of Your Life.* New York: Time Warner Book Group, 2005.

Stone, Howard W. *Defeating Depression: Real Help for You and Those Who Love You.* Minneapolis, Minn.: Augsburg Fortress Publishers, 2007.

Tristan, Kathryn. *Anxiety Rescue: Simple Strategies to Stop Fear From Ruling Your Life.* Chesterfield, Mo.: Dancing Eagle Press, 2007.

Wood, Jeffrey C. *Getting Help: The Complete and Authoritative Guide to Self-Assessment & Treatment of Mental Health Problems.* Oakland, Calif.: New Harbinger Publications, 2007.

# Index

## A

Abixa 85

abject fear 39

acetylcholine 50

acetylcholinesterase 50

acquired immunodeficiency syndrome (AIDS) 28

Adderall 14

addiction
  to antianxiety prescription medications 76, 77
  to antidepressants 17, 77
  to benzodiazepines 15, 22, 24–25
  to meprobamate 24

adenosine triphosphate (ATP) 66

ADHD. *See* attention-deficit/hyperactivity disorder

adrenal glands 34

adrenaline (epinephrine) 14, 33

Afghanistan War 33

agoraphobia 41

AIDS (acquired immunodeficiency syndrome) 28

Akatinol 85

alcoholism 23, 39

alpha-methylphenethylamine 14

alprazolam (Xanax) 23, 25, 63, *76,* 77, 82

Ambien (zolpidem) 23, 25

α-amino-3-hydroxyl-5-methyl-4-isoxazole-proprionate (AMPA) 81

amitriptyline (Elavil) 14, 17, 19, *19*

amphetamines 14, 17

Anna O. 60

antianxiety agents (anxiolytics) 23

antianxiety drugs 13–14
  abuse of 76–77
  current research on 80–82
  functioning of 52–54
  history of 22–25
  side effects of *53*
  for treatment of generalized anxiety disorder 38
  types of 15

antidepressants 13–14
  cost of 74
  current research on 80–82
  functioning of 51–52
  history of 17–22
  and neurotransmitters 27
  side effects of *53*
  and suicidal thoughts 56
  for treatment of generalized anxiety disorder 38
  types of 14–15

antiemetics 25

antihistamines 20

anxiety 12–13
  adults with *32*
  causes of 30–32
  chronic 63
  and depression 10
  emergency treatment of 62–63

anxiety attacks 62

anxiety disorders. *See also specific disorders*
  adults with *32*
  and brain biochemistry 36
  costs of 10, 28, 74–76, *75*
  effect on others 70–73
  genetic factors in 36
  personality and development of 30, 36–37
  prevalance rates of *42,* 71
  as societal problem 73
  statistics on 10

anxiolytics 23

Apresoline (hydralazine) 51

Ashwagandha 66

aspartic acid (aspartate) 50

Ativan (lorazepam) 23, 25

ATP (adenosine triphosphate) 66

attention-deficit/hyperactivity disorder (ADHD) 21, 64

Australia 29, 30–31

avoidance 34, 35, 39, 41

axons *48, 49*

axon terminals *48, 49*

Axura 85

AZD2327 (experimental drug) 85–86

## B

Baeyer, Adolf von 22

barbital 22

barbiturates 22, 23, 52, 63, 77

barbituric acid 22

Beck, Aaron T. 59

# About the Author

**Dr. Alan I. Hecht** is a practicing chiropractor in New York. He is also an adjunct professor at Farmingdale State College and Nassau Community College and an adjunct associate professor at the C.W. Post campus of Long Island University. He teaches courses in medical microbiology, anatomy and physiology, comparative anatomy, human physiology, embryology, and general biology. In addition, he is the course coordinator for Human Biology at Hofstra University where he is an adjunct assistant professor.

Dr. Hecht received his B.S. in Biology–Pre-Medical Studies from Fairleigh Dickinson University in Teaneck, New Jersey. He received his M.S. in Basic Medical Sciences from New York University School of Medicine. He also received his Doctor of Chiropractic (D.C.) degree from New York Chiropractic College in Brookville, New York.

# About the Consulting Editor

Consulting editor **David J. Triggle, Ph.D.**, is a SUNY Distinguished Professor and the University Professor at the State University of New York at Buffalo. These are the two highest academic ranks of the university. Professor Triggle received his education in the United Kingdom with a Ph.D. degree in chemistry at the University of Hull. Following post-doctoral fellowships at the University of Ottawa (Canada) and the University of London (United Kingdom) he assumed a position in the School of Pharmacy at the University at Buffalo. He served as chairman of the Department of Biochemical Pharmacology from 1971 to 1985 and as Dean of the School of Pharmacy from 1985 to 1995. From 1996 to 2001 he served as Dean of the Graduate School and from 1999 to 2001 was also the University Provost. He is currently the University Professor, in which capacity he teaches bioethics and science policy, and is President of the Center for Inquiry Institute, a think tank located in Amherst, New York and devoted to issues around the public understanding of science. In the latter respect he is a major contributor to the online M.Ed. program—"Science and The Public"—in the Graduate School of Education and The Center for Inquiry.